SIN, DEATH, AND THE DEVIL

Sin, Death, and the Devil

Edited by

Carl E. Braaten and Robert W. Jenson

William B. Eerdmans Publishing Company
Grand Rapids, Michigan / Cambridge, U.K.

© 2000 Wm. B. Eerdmans Publishing Co.
255 Jefferson Ave. S.E., Grand Rapids, Michigan 49503 /
P.O. Box 163, Cambridge CB3 9PU U.K.

Printed in the United States of America

05 04 03 02 01 00   7 6 5 4 3 2 1

Library of Congress Cataloging-in-Publication Data

Sin, death, and the Devil / edited by Carl E. Braaten and Robert W. Jenson.
    p.   cm.
    Includes bibliographical references.
    ISBN 0-8028-4695-5 (pbk.: alk. paper)
    1. Sin. 2. Death — Religious aspects — Christianity. 3. Devil.
  I. Braaten, Carl E., 1929- II. Jenson, Robert W.

BT715 S63 2000
241′.3 — dc21   99-052508

Contents

Introduction:
Much Ado about Nothingness

ROBERT W. JENSON

We cannot deny it: the negatives came first. No one at this end of modernity and of history's bloodiest century can think seriously about either church or world without apprehending the actuality of the classic biblical tyrants; and the Center for Catholic and Evangelical Theology has from its inception been dedicated to serious thought. Sin, death, and devil have therefore been much on our minds. Indeed, John Paul II's description of a "culture of death" provided the original germ of planning for the conference at which all but one of the following papers were delivered and discussed.

But we quickly decided it would not do to give such mere nihilities (to steal Karl Barth's coinage) even so much reality as to follow their lead in structuring our conference. So, despite the title, it is the sacraments of God's victory over the tyrants that shaped the conference and this book. There are three pairs of papers; within each pair is one on a sacrament and one on the tyrant it most specifically undoes. A seventh paper became available and fits so well that we decided to include it.

For indeed God's opponents share one defining feature: since they are not willed by God, indeed are his opponents, their ontological status is nil, and it is to that point that this introductory essay will be devoted. The only question about the devil is what ails him; sin is always a rejection of the good; and death is of course a sudden absence.

Sin first. Since history is mostly made by our sinning, one might suppose that sin must be a very active thing. But the theological tradi-

1

tion is nearly unanimous in perceiving that sin's apparent agency is a fraud. History's whole dismal armory of sins, so impressive from a distance, is only a selection of ways *not* to be one thing, righteous. We are created to be righteous, that is, to form one community with each other and with the persons of the triune God, in which each of us takes her or his unique place and uses that place as an opportunity to love the rest of us. Any sin humanity can think of is simply one or another way of refusing to do this.

Indeed, since our location within the triune life and with each other is our very being, since I exist at all only in that I am given a location at which to serve community, sin is always a diminution of being, a declension from reality. St. Augustine set the terms of Western theology in this matter when he conceived all being as a sort of ladder, with the refulgent being of God at the top and the darkness of sheer nothingness at the bottom, and conceived sin as any movement of the soul by which she directs herself downward instead of upward. To sin is to achieve precisely . . . nothing.

And then there is death. Death is a double negativity.

Death is impossible to conceive, and not just because we are reluctant to face it. Late modernity has generally supposed it brave to say that death is the simple cessation of the person; and apart from the gospel this supposition would doubtless be the part of valor. Historically, however, humanity has found the sheer cessation of a person literally unthinkable, for death so conceived is the termination of consciousness, and that turns out to be an impossible thought.

I can, of course, affirm and as a matter of mere language understand the proposition, "My consciousness will some day cease." But if I try to summon what Hegel called a "representation," that is, a depiction of possible experience to go with the proposition, all I can conjure is a consciousness of darkness and emptiness or the strange consciousness of sleep, all of which of course are still consciousness. Moreover, the present nothingness of a consciousness would be constituted by memory: I, the erstwhile such-an-one, am nothing. Thus when I try to think my own death simply as cessation, the best I can do is to think of myself as remembering that I used to be and so being conscious that I now am nothing and am conscious of nothing. To the concept of truly vanished consciousness, no projected experience, no representation, can correspond.

There is perhaps one way in which I can think the cessation of my consciousness: I can try to think general nonexistence. For to abolish consciousness, we must abolish not only immediate present perception, but memory and anticipation as well. With respect to any particular consciousness, its extinction is therefore exactly the same as there never having been or being or going to be anything at all; nor does this merely mean that for that consciousness it is the same *as if* there had been nothing at all. The vanishing of a consciousness is the — even retrospective! — non-existence of the world.

Israel had a clearer grasp of this matter than other nations, just because she had a clearer grasp of life itself. Indeed, Israel's grasp of death was a sheer refusal to grasp it at all.

For pre-exilic Israel, the dead are shadows of former selves, resident in the grave as a realm of what precisely *used to be*. In Israel, this conception left what Gerhard von Rad called a "theologically strange vacuum" in her interpretation of reality, a negative fact not interpreted by Exodus or creation, and so not within the Lord's domain: a psalmist could presume that "those who go down to the Pit . . . you remember no more, for they are cut off from your hand." This psalmist's question, "Is your steadfast love declared in the grave . . . , or your saving help in the land of forgetfulness?", was intended as bitter rhetoric — though it is open to a different answer than his, which in time was given.

And finally there is that incarnation of vacuity, the devil. Karl Barth puzzled normal minds by saying that the devil was a myth. Folk were alarmed: Barth, they said, doesn't believe in the devil. But of course that was just the point: one believes in God, and in another sense in such things as salvation, and just possibly sometimes in other persons or even in certain facts about the world, but assuredly not in the devil. Barth's point was that *not* believing in the devil is the appropriate relation to the devil's mode of existence. That the devil is a myth doesn't mean, in Barth's thinking, that he doesn't exist; it means that he exists in a particular way, as the ordained object of denial.

Putting it my way, the only description possible of the devil is a description of what is the matter with him. The only predicates of the devil are his deficiencies, for the devil is the angel who refuses to be one.

So — the common reality of all faith's adversaries is their nothingness. And that is to say that the permanent opposite of faith is *nihilism*, the position that takes sin, death, and the devil as the final truth. Nihilism believes in nothing because it believes there is nothing to cling to, and so clinging to nothing is all there is — and if the move from the one to the other is a logical fallacy, that too is part of the matter.

Nihilism is the specifically Christian opposite possibility. It is not possible for the fallen natural man to be a nihilist, because he is too captive to idolatry, to worshipping the creature instead of the Creator, and so, of course, to worshipping something or other.

The creature is available on our terms, as the Creator is not. So long as we worship the creature instead of the Creator, so long as the creature is for us the ground of its own being and of ours, the ground of being seems to be right there available to us, and the nihilistic suspicion does not arise; there *is* divinity, available for our invocation; Father Sun and Mother Earth and all the rest are visibly up and down there, and that is that. But when we know that the creatures are not divine, that the ground of the creatures — if any — is a Creator not immediately available, and if moroever that Creator is presented to us in a despised nation and a crucified man, then room opens for the fear that being may be groundless. The threatening nihilism of late modernity is specific to a culture that *used to be* Christian.

The story of the West's secularization precisely by the Bible has been told so often that I do not need again to rehearse it at any length. Where the Bible comes, the creatures are stripped of their pretenses to divinity. Neither Jews nor Christians are permitted to "bow down to the host of heaven," or invoke spirits, or luxuriate in the great Goddess's Earth-womb. For the Lord is first, last, and foremost a jealous God, the Creator who tolerates no creaturely pretensions to be other than creatures.

In Tom Stoppard's great play, *Jumpers,* a chief character is a torch singer who abandons her career when men walk on the moon. How can one sing of Aphrodite, the divine power of Romance, when clumsy men in funny suits are trampling about on the goddess?

But what if a culture, having under the impact of the Bible become unable to worship the creature, then ceases to believe there is a Creator? Then there is precisely nothing to believe in. And that, it seems, is what our culture is coming to.

This does not mean there is not all manner of desperate scurrying around, for religious figleaves to cover nothingness. So in the bookstores under "religion" the celestial calendars of archaic civilizations appear again, teaching how properly to reverence the host of heaven.

The shamans, once known as "witch doctors," reappear as gurus to the middle-class. The great Goddess, Mother Earth, is once again worshipped — sort of.

But we should not be deceived: the postmodern return to paganism is a fake. That is, it is nihilism redoubled, emptiness trying to cover itself with pretense known, deep down, to be pretense. Late-modern re-evocations of paganism are not *serious*: their devotees know that the heavenly bodies, however bizarre, are of the same matter as we; that Mother Earth cannot actually be impregnated; that fucking in the furrows, however deliciously transgressive, will not increase the harvest. It is all empty; it is about . . . nothing. We will know that the great Goddess is really back when "re-imaging" conferences feature temple prostitution and mass male castration to provide priests; until then, prattle about the Goddess, celebrated with children's ring-games, in fact reduces the terrible old deity to triviality, in fact secularizes her yet again.

So what is the pay-off of this diagnosis of our situation? Two steps, and I am done.

The first step is the serious one. Surely it is important for the church to know the opposition. Whether actual nihilism, flat-out disbelief in everything, is a real human possibility, remains perhaps to be seen. But the *threat* of nihilism is the defining evil from which the church has to rescue the inhabitants of Western late modernity.

Why cannot our nation, and indeed the people of our churches, rid themselves of the horror of infant slaughter on demand, and perhaps soon of senior-citizen slaughter on demand? Because, I suggest, Americans finally do not know how to distinguish human persons from the beasts of the field, because they are unwitting anthropological nihilists.

Why could not our people summon any moral outrage about a corrupt and indeed quite openly nihilistic president? Early in the Monica-saga, there was a television interview with a young man-in-the-street. He was pleased with the news, since it showed that someone just like him could become president.

Why cannot we have good schools, except where the church or heroic or charismatic individuals maintain them? Because, I suggest, the culture at large has precisely *nothing* to teach.

What ails Christians in this nation and this time, and ails also those who fancy themselves and indeed are called to be leaders of the faithful, is the infiltration of nihilism, the infiltration of that mere nothingness which sin, death, and the devil have in common, and which emerges in its own nonentity in an ex-Christian culture.

Nihilism is one enemy we cannot co-opt. Nothingness is just that, a black hole of being, and like an astronomical black hole sucks in everything that approaches it. Accommodation to the empty thud of late-modern pop music, to the short attention span of the baby boomers, to decadent Americanism's horror of distinctions and decisions, will only further damage the souls of those the church pursues by such accommodation. Pastors and church leaders in our time must be wary indeed, lest *we* turn out to be nihilism's agents.

The second step is serious too, but only in its specific way. There is nothing more suited to levity than nothing; laughter is finally the necessary response to anything pretending to be what it is not. In the case of our three villains and their joint nihility, laughter is the doubly necessary response to nothing pretending to be something. Luther famously threw an inkwell at the devil, and people have always thought the story funny — and that, of course, is the point. You can't throw an inkwell at the devil. Why not? Because wherever he is he isn't! And there have been few guides for the avoidance of evil as effective as C. S. Lewis's *Screwtape Letters*. It is notorious: the devil cannot stand to be laughed at, because laughter reveals that this emperor not only has no clothes but doesn't even have a self to wear clothes if he had any.

As to sin, let us take sexual sin for our example. There is no telling how many persons, in the grip of a supposedly overwhelming grand passion and about to throw family and faith and integrity to the winds for its sake, have been saved by recall of the great quip that the pleasure is fleeting, the cost exorbitant, and the position ridiculous. And even as to death, its terrorism is for those in Christ's care pompous to the point of hilarity: the author of this introduction will indulge in just so much personal self-revelation as to say that when I wake in the night sure my coronary hour has come, I usually resist all Blanche's attempts to save me from my terrors — also by quoting my own theology to me — until she threatens actually to call 911 and evokes the image of arriving at the emergency ward to have my heart attack there, "presenting," as they say, the feeling that it has to happen sometime so why not tonight?

The sacraments overcome the tyrants. God's sacraments are real, and the tyrants finally are not. So go ahead: it's safe to read this book.

Sinsick

STANLEY HAUERWAS

> People are religious to the extent that they believe themselves to be not so much *imperfect,* as ill. Any man who is halfway decent will think himself extremely imperfect, but a religious man thinks himself *wretched.*
>
> Ludwig Wittgenstein, *Culture and Value* (45e)

1. Sickness as Sin

Given the choice, most people in America would rather be sick than a sinner. Sin sounds too judgmental for a "compassionate culture." Sickness has become our way to indicate deviancy without blame. Karl Menninger lamented this development in his book, *Whatever Became of Sin?* He acknowledged, however, that his attempt to rehabilitate the language of sin is not for the sake of the word itself, "but for the reintroduction of the concepts of guilt and moral responsibility."[1] It is ironic, therefore, that many conservative Christians were sympathetic with Menninger's effort to reclaim sin, not only because his account of sin drew on those conceptions derived from Protestant liberalism, that is, Tillich and Reinhold Niebuhr, but because his conception was

---

1. Karl Menninger, *Whatever Became of Sin?* (New York: Hawthorn Books, 1973), 48.

hopelessly moralistic.[2] What could be more sinful than the presumption that our guilt might tell us something interesting about our sin? Guilt is, after all, just an invitation to self-righteousness.

Yet sin and sickness are not easily distinguished; but distinguish them we must. I believe sickness is a manifestation of sin, but how to say that without inviting false theodical speculations is difficult. Indeed in our time the discovery that we are sick is often the nearest analogy we have for understanding what it means to discover and confess we are sinners. Alcoholics discover they are possessed by a power they do not remember choosing but for which they must take responsibility if they are to stand any chance of being free from that possession. In like manner Christians confess that they are sinners. Sin, like sickness, seems more like something that happens to us than what we do. Yet as Christians we believe that we are rightly held accountable for our sins.

Before exploring how sickness manifests our sin I need to make clear why for most people the language of being sick seems more intelligible than being a sinner. I think the answer is very simple — we are atheists. Even if we say we believe in God, most of our lives are constituted by practices that assume that God does not exist. The most effective means I have discovered to illustrate this is to ask people how they want to die. We all want to die quickly, painlessly, in our sleep, and without being a burden. We do not want to be a burden because we can no longer trust our children. We want to die quickly, painlessly, and in our sleep because when we die we do not want to know we are dying.

It is quite interesting to contrast this with the past, when the death Christians feared was a sudden death. They feared a sudden death because such a death meant they might die unreconciled with their neighbors, their church, and, of course, God. We no longer fear the judgment of God, but we do fear death. So our lives are lived in an attempt to avoid death (or at least the knowledge that we are to die) as long as we can. As any doctor can tell you, sickness is the intimation of death — even hangnails. Accordingly we order our lives to be free of sickness. But so ordered, sickness becomes overdetermined as

2. For an extensive critique of liberal accounts of sin, see "Salvation Even in Sin: Learning to Speak Truthfully About Ourselves," in my book, *Sanctify Them in the Truth: Holiness Exemplified* (Edinburgh: T. & T. Clark, 1998), 61-76.

a description that indicates any aspect of our lives that threatens death. Growing old turns out, therefore, to be an illness.

This set of presumptions, of course, has resulted in giving extraordinary power to the medical profession. The hospitals at Duke, Duke North and Duke South, are like the cathedrals of the past — our Chartres and Notre Dames that testify not as those cathedrals did to what we love but rather are testimonies to what we fear. As I often point out to seminarians, if you want some idea of what medieval Christianity felt like, hang around any modern research medical center. The description "Byzantine" fails to do justice to the complex forms of power exercised in such a context. Nowhere is such power more manifest than the ability of those in medicine to extend their power by redescribing our lives through the language of illness. Thus we are now being taught that "baldness" is a condition that we can "cure."

That medicine has such power is one of the reasons medical schools are more morally impressive than, for example, divinity schools. When challenged about where schools of virtue may exist, I often say Paris Island and/or medical schools. For example, a person can come to divinity school today saying, "I am not really into Christology this year. I am really into relating. I would like to take more courses in CPE." They are likely to be confirmed in that option by being told, "Right, take CPE, after all that is what ministry is — relating. Learn to be a wounded healer."

Contrast that with a medical student who might say, "I am not really into anatomy this year. I am really into people. I would like to take another course in psychiatry." They would be told, "We do not care what you are 'into.' Take anatomy or ship out." That is real moral education if not formation. Why is medical education so morally superior to ministerial education? I think the answer is very simple. No one believes that an inadequately trained priest might damage their salvation; but people do believe that an inadequately trained doctor might hurt them.

It is a mistake, moreover, to blame physicians for having such power over our lives. They simply reflect who we are. In many ways those in medicine suffer from our determination to redescribe our lives in the language of sickness. For example, we now expect doctors to keep us alive to the point that when we die we do not have to know we are dying. We then get to blame doctors for keeping us alive to no point. Physicians are as a result sued for doing too much or too little to "cure us" because they now serve patients who have no sense of the limits of medicine. Patients have forgotten what every doctor knows, namely, that the final description for every patient for which a physician cares is "dead."[3]

I think it would be a mistake to think the overdetermination of the language of sickness in our culture to be a conspiracy by those in medicine to acquire power. On the contrary, I believe patient and physician alike manifest the fundamental presumption of liberal social orders that assume freedom to be not only the ideal but the necessary condition for moral and political life. As I am fond of putting the matter, the project of modernity has been to produce people who believe they should have no story other than the story they chose when they had no story. Of course what such a story cannot explain is how that story became our story. In short, modernity names those social orders in which freedom became our fate.

As a result we suffer from those forms of life we believe necessary to make us free. We desire to be free from illness, and illness is now understood as any condition that limits our choices. Sickness names those aspects of our lives we have not chosen. This creates the desire of modern people to find the "cause" of their illness in some "lifestyle" choice because such a "cause" at least makes their suffering intelligible. That is why the illness and death of children, which is a challenge for any time and people, is a particular challenge for us.[4] Medicine is the institutionalized practice we have formed to free us from the surdness of sickness and death that now threaten to tyrannize our lives. That we have now become subject to the power of medicine is not the fault of doctors and others in health care professions, but rather the reflection of our inability to make sense that we are creatures destined to die. Put bluntly, we are unable to make sense of our being sick because we no longer understand what it means for our lives to be captured by sin.

---

3. For reflection on the patience that should be required of Christian patients, see Charles Pinches and Stanley Hauerwas, *Christians Among the Virtues: Theological Conversations with Ancient and Modern Ethics* (Notre Dame: University of Notre Dame Press, 1997), 166-178.

4. This is the issue I tried to explore in *God, Medicine, and Suffering* (Grand Rapids: Eerdmans, 1994). The original title was *Naming the Silences*.

2. Sinsick

In fact we are sinsick. I learned to use the word sinsick by singing (God knows how many times) "There Is a Balm in Gilead."[5] That balm, it turns out, can "cleanse the sinsick soul." Sinsick was one of those "Southern" expressions we used "down home" to describe someone who was on his or her last leg. To describe people as sinsick meant their life was in shambles involving both physical and spiritual conditions. We presumed that sickness and sin could not be separated though we did not assume an exact causality. Rather sickness itself was regarded as part of our natural condition given that our natural condition was one of sin. We knew we had not been created to be sinners, but we knew that's what we were — namely, a people quite literally made sick by sin.

I think the presumption we are made sick by sin is theologically right no matter how much it may offend our sensibilities. Moreover, I think that is also what the church has taught; or at least, it is what Aquinas taught. Aquinas simply assumes that sickness, and the death sickness intimates, was the result of sin. Of course, Aquinas thought his account of sin and sickness was but commentary on Paul's claim in Romans (5:12) that "by one man sin entered into this world, and by sin death." Responding to the objection that death and other bodily defects are not the result of sin, Aquinas observes:

> As death and such like defects are beside the intention of the sinner, it is evident that sin is not, of itself, the cause of these defects. Accidently one thing is the cause of another if it causes it by removing an obstacle: thus it is stated in *Phys.* viii, 32, that "by displacing a pillar a man moves accidentally the stone resting thereon." In this way the sin of our first parent is the cause of death and all such like defects in human nature, in so far as by the sin of our first parent original justice was taken away, whereby not only were the lower powers of the soul held together under the control of reason, without any disorder whatever, but also the whole body was held together in subjection to the soul, without any defect. Wherefore, original justice being forfeited through the sin of our first parent; just as human nature was

5. I am indebted to my colleague and friend Richard Hays for reminding me that "sinsick" is used in the hymn, "There Is a Balm in Gilead." This proves the description was not peculiar to Texas, because Richard is from Oklahoma.

stricken in the soul by the disorder among the powers, so also it became subject to corruption, by reason of disorder in the body. Now the withdrawal of original justice has the character of punishment, even as the withdrawal of grace has. Consequently, death and all consequent bodily defects are punishments of original sin, and although the defects are not intended by the sinner, nevertheless they are ordered to the justice of God who inflicts them as punishments.[6]

In an earlier article on whether original sin infects the will before the other powers, Aquinas observed that original sin is like an infection. In fact he compares it to leprosy. It spreads from the flesh to the soul and then from the essence of the soul to the powers. The infection is most apparent in those aspects of our lives that are not subject to reason such as the "members of generation" that serve for the "mingling of sexes." The concupiscible and the sense of touch are also among our faculties most subject to original sin since they are subject to transmission from one subject to another.[7]

Aquinas's understanding of the effect of sin can only be understood against the background of his view that we were not created to die. He quotes *Wisdom* 1:13, "Now God made not death," and concludes that death is not natural to man.[8] The position of Aquinas about the naturalness of our deaths is, however, quite complex. As regards our form — that is, our rational soul — death is not, according to Aquinas, natural to man. But the matter of man, which is our body, is composed of contraries, "of which corruptibility is a necessary consequence, and in this respect death is natural to man." Aquinas illustrates this claim by providing an example of a craftsman, who if he could would make a saw that at once would be hard enough to cut but would not rust. So God, who is the all-powerful author of man, when "He first made man, He conferred on him the favor of being exempt from the necessity resulting from such matter: which favor, however, was withdrawn through the sin of our first parents. Accordingly death is both natural on account of a condition attaching to matter and penal on account of the loss of the Divine favor preserving man from death."[9]

6. Thomas Aquinas, *Summa Theologica*, translated by Fathers of the English Dominican Province (Westminster, MD: Christian Classics, 1948), I-II, 85, 5.

7. Aquinas, *Summa Theologica*, I-II, 84, 2.

8. Aquinas, *Summa Theologica*, I-II, 85, 1.

9. Aquinas, *Summa Theologica*, II-II, 164, 2.

Interestingly enough, Aquinas does not think that the first sin was in the flesh, because "man was so appointed in the state of innocence, that there was no rebellion of the flesh against the spirit." Rather, the first sin was our prideful and inordinate desiring of a spiritual good that Aquinas identifies as the desire to be like God. Of course, our first parents could not have desired absolute equality with God since such a likeness is not conceivable to the mind. Rather, the first man desired knowledge of good and evil; that is, he desired by his own natural power to determine what was good and what was evil for him to do.[10] Such a desire had the effect of disordering our lives so that we became subject to death and disease.

In our primitive state God had bestowed his favor on man so that man's mind was subject to God and the lower powers of the soul were subject to the rational mind and the body to the soul. But through sin man's mind was no longer subject to God with the result that man's lower powers were no longer subject to his reason.

> Whence there followed so great a rebellion of the carnal appetite against the reason; nor was the body wholly subject to the soul; whence arose death and other bodily defects. For life and soundness of body depend on the body being subject to the soul, as the perfectible is subject to its perfection. Consequently, on the other hand, death, sickness, and all defects of the body are due to the lack of the body's subjection to the soul.[11]

The punishment of death and sickness was proportionate to the first sin insofar as they are the result of the withdrawal of Divine favor necessary for the rectitude and integrity of human nature. These punishments, however, need not be equal in those to whom the first sin appertains. But since God foreknows all future events, God, according to Aquinas, providentially apportioned these penalties in different ways to different people. Aquinas argues that this is not, as Origen held, on account of merits or demerits of a previous life because such a view would be contrary to the words of Romans 9:11, "When they . . . had not done any good or evil." Moreover, Origen's view falsely assumes the soul was created before the body. Rather, such punishments are for parents' sins since the child belongs to the parents, and

---

10. Aquinas, *Summa Theologica*, II-II, 163, 1-2.
11. Aquinas, *Summa Theologica*, II-II, 164, 1.

parents are thus often punished in their children. Or penalty is as a "remedy intended for the spiritual welfare of the person who suffers these penalties, to wit that he may thus be turned away from his sins, or lest he take pride in his virtues, and that he may be crowned for his patience."[12]

Aquinas does not presume that everything we might regard as unpleasant is the result of the fall. He observes, for example, that even prior to the first sin man was the head and governor of the woman. Sin transforms that relation into punishment, as now the woman must obey her husband against her will. In like manner thorns and thistles would have existed to provide food for animals prior to the fall. Only after the fall do they become punishment, making our labor more difficult.[13] I think it is not hard to see that Aquinas thinks the body, which was destined to die, analogous to thorns and thistles.

How Aquinas thinks about these matters is wonderfully illustrated in his discussion in the Third Part of the *Summa* where he speculates on the integrity of the body in the resurrection. For example, he answers the question of whether all the parts of the human body will rise again by noting that since the resurrection is the work of God, and since the works of God are perfect, in the resurrection man will be made perfect in all his members. Just as a work of art would not be perfect if its product lacked any of the things that are contained in the art, so "at the resurrection it behooves man's body to correspond entirely to the soul, for it will not rise again except according to the relation it bears to the rational soul, it follows that man also must rise again perfect, seeing that he is thereby repaired in order that he may obtain his ultimate perfection. Consequently all the members that are now in man's body must needs be restored at the resurrection."[14]

If we have lost a hand or a leg during our life — even if the member was cut off before a person repented and, therefore, did not cooperate with him in the state whereby he merits glory — yet, according to Aquinas, we will be restored whole since it is the whole being that serves God. Moreover, we will also be raised at the height of our powers since Christ rose at a youthful age, that is, around thirty, and so we will also be raised. It is appropriate for us to be raised at the most per-

12. Aquinas, *Summa Theologica*, II-II, 164, 1, 4.
13. Aquinas, *Summa Theologica*, II-II, 164, 2.
14. Aquinas, *Summa Theologica*, Q. 80, Art. 1, Supplement.

fect stage of nature, and human nature is most perfect in the age of youth, so we will be raised at that age.[15] I regret to report that the only slip Aquinas made in his discussion of our resurrected state involved a misreading of Luke 21:18 where we are told not a hair of our head shall perish. Aquinas comments: "Hair and nails were given to man as an ornament. Now the bodies of men, especially of the elect, ought to rise again with all their adornment. Therefore they ought to rise again with the hair."[16]

That we — that is, people schooled on the presumption that sickness and sin are not related — find Aquinas's discussion of these matters somewhat bizarre, I take to be an indication of the pathology of the modern soul. "Sickness" for us, as I noted above, is pointless. Being "sick" is a condition that should not exist and thereby justifies unlimited interventions to eliminate what we regard as an arbitrary inconvenience. Yet sickness was not "pointless" for Aquinas, but rather an indication of the distorting effect sin has in our lives. We were not created to be sick or to die, but because we discover our lives are unavoidably constituted by death and sickness, we have an indication something terrible has gone wrong. We are sinsick.

Aquinas says no more than what Christians are bound to say about sickness and death. The problem, of course, is that saying these things sounds like such bad news to modern ears. Death and sickness so narrated appear to make God a divine sadist arbitrarily punishing his creatures in an effort to get minimal respect. Yet I believe Aquinas's account to be the exact opposite of such a reading since the discovery of sin and death are part of the good news that we were not created to die. Moreover, Aquinas's way of framing our understanding of sin, sickness, and death I believe offers exactly the kind of discriminations necessary to sustain a practice of medicine that will not be driven mad by its inability to cure. In order to show how this might be the case I need to develop why the discovery we are sinners is part of the good news of the gospel.

---

15. Aquinas, *Summa Theologica*, Q. 81, Art. 1, Suppl.
16. Aquinas, *Summa Theologica*, Q. 80, Art. 2, Suppl.

3. The Joy of Being Sick[17]

> As he walked along, he saw a man blind from birth. His disciples
> asked him, "Rabbi, who sinned, this man or his parents, that he was
> born blind?" Jesus answered, "Neither this man nor his parents
> sinned; he was born blind so that God's works might be revealed in
> him."

This passage from the ninth chapter of John is the appropriate place
for Christians to reflect on sin, sickness, and death. As James Alison
points out, in the encounter between Jesus and this blind man we
have a meditation on how Jesus' life and resurrection transforms our
understanding of sin as well as the relation of sin and sickness.[18]
Moreover, Jesus' treatment of the man born blind is a wonderful indication that while sickness is the result of our sin, it is usually a mistake to correlate a person's sickness with a particular sin.

Alison observes that the story of Jesus' healing of the man born
blind is one of inclusion and exclusion. The blind man is excluded
not only from the good of seeing, but also from full participation in
the cultic life of Israel since his blindness was considered a moral
impediment. Jesus uses the resources of the original creation, that
is, clay mixed with his own spittle, to cure the man's blindness even
though it is on the Sabbath. The man is sent to a pool to wash, a
place of purification, making possible the reintegration of the man
born blind, intimating for us the baptism to be ours through resurrection.

Yet the man is not accepted back into Israel since the Pharisees
rightly realize that the cure unavoidably requires acknowledgment of
the messianic nature of Jesus' ministry. So they throw the blind man
out. During the process, however, the former blind man, who had
never seen Jesus because he only received his sight at the pool of
Siloam, becomes increasingly aware of who Jesus is: first just another
man, then a prophet, and finally he is someone from God who is superior even to Moses. Like the disciples, who also must be trained to see

---

17. This subtitle is a play on a title of James Alison's *The Joy of Being Wrong: Original
Sin Through Easter Eyes* (New York: Crossroad Herder Book, 1998). It will become obvi-
ous how much I owe Alison's quite extraordinary presentation for the general argument
of this paper.

18. Alison discusses this passage in *The Joy of Being Wrong* on pp. 120-125.

through discipleship, so the man born blind comes to see who Jesus is by being rejected.

"For judgment I came into the world, that those who do not see may see, and that those who see may become blind," is Jesus' final judgment on this proceeding. Yet Alison rightly comments that this is ironic since Jesus makes no active judgment in the narrative. Rather it is the Pharisees who judge by casting out the man born blind. Alison suggests this is the Johannine recasting of judgment — by being crucified Jesus is the real judge of his judges. Jesus does not abolish the notion of judgment but as judge subverts from within the notion of those who would judge; that is, the judgment that excludes the blind man is revealed as the judgment that those who would expel are blind.

Alison's reading of John 9 substantiates the argument he makes throughout *The Joy of Being Wrong* that "the doctrine of original sin is not prior to, but follows from and is utterly dependent on, Jesus' resurrection from the dead and thus cannot be understood at all except in the light of that event."[19] This revolution in the concept of sin is achieved in the life of this man born blind, Alison argues, because John quite rightly applies to what is without doubt one of Jesus' historical healings the understanding of sin made possible by the resurrection. The sin of the world is understood, following from John 8:44 as the work of "your father the devil," who "was a murderer from the beginning." That reign of sin has now been overturned, making possible a new creation embodied in a community that is at once as old and new as creation. As Alison puts it:

> When Jesus speaks, at the end, about judgment it is clear that he is not concerned with a particular local incident, but about a discernment relating to the whole world *(kosmos)*. Here we have a highly subtle teaching about the whole world being blind from birth, from the beginning, and about Jesus, in the light of the world coming to bring sight to the world, being rejected precisely by those who, though blind, claimed to be able to see. All humans are blind, but where this blindness is compounded by active participation in the mechanisms of exclusion pretending to sight, this blindness is culpable.[20]

19. Alison, *Joy of Being Wrong*, 3.
20. Alison, *Joy of Being Wrong*, 123.

The doctrine of original sin, according to Alison, is good news
made possible only by Christ's resurrection.[21] The doctrine of original
sin is not an accusation against humanity, and by keeping the doctrine
alive the Church is not engaged in a generalized condemnation of humanity. Rather what is at stake in the doctrine of original sin is the
possibility "that even those who bear the tremendous burden of being
'right' may recognize their complicity with those who are not, and so
construct a sociality that is not cruciform."[22] So understood, what the
doctrine of original sin or any account of sin cannot be is an explanation for evil or suffering. Original sin does not "explain" death and
sickness because, as Alison puts it, the Catholic faith is not an explanation for anything. Rather than an explanation the church has a
salvific revelation:

> What is revealed as something now operative is the mystery of God's
> plan of salvation for us. This plan of salvation enables us to know the
> Father and share in his life by sharing in the life and death of his Son.
> Any Catholic understanding of evil cannot be part of a general human
> understanding of evil, and this for two reasons. In the first place there
> is no such thing as a general human understanding of evil any more
> than there is a general human understanding of good. It is contingent
> and competing human traditions that give shape and form to differing
> notions of good and evil, and such traditions all carry with them, ei-

---

21. I cannot here develop Alison's quite extraordinary Christology except to say I
am in deep sympathy with his insistence on the historical and bodily character of salvation. Alison rightly assumes the salvation wrought by God in Christ is contingent,
which means "that salvation works precisely at the level of producing a different social
other, through contingent historical acts and texts, with physical relations, signs and so
on. This, of course, places us on a somewhat different course from any transcendental
anthropology, which sees, as a matter of philosophical truth, the human being as im-
bued with a somehow experienced orientation toward grace and glory and therefore the
concrete, contingent, historical acts of salvation (the prophets, the coming of Christ,
the existence of the Church, the sacraments) as merely making explicit the universal
availability of grace." Following this claim Alison notes he does not want to deny that
all humans are by the fact of being human called to participate in the divine life. "However, it seems to me that this *theological* doctrine is an important human discovery made
in the light of the death and resurrection of Jesus of Nazareth and is part of a discovery
that we are, in fact, quite different from what we normally think we are. That is to say,
the doctrine of the universal vocation to *theiosis* is itself part of the discovery of salvation
as a difficult process worked out in hope, in which we hope to become something which
we are not, or are scarcely, now" (42-43).

22. Alison, *Joy of Being Wrong*, 261.

ther explicitly or implicitly, a theology that undergirds them. Secondly, the Catholic faith considers itself radically subversive of all forms of human knowledge (I Cor. 1:18-25) because of a very peculiar epistemological starting point: the resurrection with historical circumstances of a murdered man as the beginnings of a new creation.[23]

Accordingly the church's approach to sin (and sickness) is not to provide an explanation, but to be a contingent human transformation whereby our condition as sinners is bounded by the more determinative reality of our salvation. Sin and sickness from the church's perspective just "are." In Alison's terms, sin for Christians is "that which we are on our way out of."[24] We must not, like Lot's wife, turn around to see that which we have left. To do so is to let sin become the primary character in the story. Moreover, when original sin becomes an explanation it too easily becomes an excuse for not overcoming evil, "a way of justifying the present state of affairs rather than being the understanding of what it is that is being overcome on our way out of it."[25]

Alison argues, rightly I think, that the account he has given of original sin as the good news made possible by the resurrection is not only consistent with Aquinas's account of these matters, but in fact *is* Aquinas's account of original sin. That Aquinas understands original sin to result in a privation of original justice makes clear that the doctrine of original sin is an ancillary concept rather than a basic one. Put differently: the story of the "fall" Christians believe to be the appropriate reading of the account of Adam and Eve in Genesis is a reading made possible only because we now understand that Jesus is the new Adam.[26]

23. Alison, *Joy of Being Wrong*, 262.

24. Alison, *Joy of Being Wrong*, 263.

25. Alison, *Joy of Being Wrong*, 170. One cannot help to think of Reinhold Niebuhr as the strongest example of such a use of original sin. For Niebuhr original sin became a generalized anthropological description used to justify the lesser of two evil arguments. Accordingly any account of holiness was undercut by the oft made Niebuhrian presumption that when all is said and done we are all sinners. Of course it is true we are all sinners. The problem is when that becomes a coverting law explanation to justify the way things are.

26. Alison, *Joy of Being Wrong*, 300. While I find Alison's account persuasive I am not convinced his contrast of the New Testament with the Old is right. I simply do not know how Jews may or may not understand how sin shapes our lives.

Such a view makes the effects of sin no less serious. We suffer from sin and the sickness that is a result of sin. It may be true that we were not created to die, but we know we continue to die deadly deaths. Yet if Aquinas and Alison are right, the great good news is that our lives do not need to be determined by sin or death. Rather through baptism our lives have been reconstituted making possible freedom from death and the threat of death so often intimated by sickness. Accordingly, sin and sickness have lost their power to dominate our lives as Christians. As a result we fear not sickness but rather can now imagine our bodies in sickness and in health to be an invitation for the care of one another. That I take to be the joy of sickness.

Accordingly those called to care for us when we are sick do so not as if our illnesses have no purpose. Rather, through baptism our lives have been reborn so that neither death nor sickness can have the last word about our care for one another. Suffering sickness can even be an opportunity to share in Christ's suffering so that the world might know that death has been defeated. Therefore the practice of medicine by Christians is not an attempt to deny death, but rather a way to be of service to one another as people who understand the death we die in this life is not our destiny.

In an extraordinary chapter entitled, "Original Sin Known in Its Ecclesial Overcoming," Alison observes that the tragedy of original sin is not that it is universal, but that by it the incapacity for universality

is revealed by the coming into being of the ecclesial hypostasis in which alone particularity is made capable of bearing universality. Original sin, the an-ecclesial hypostasis, is simultaneously incapable of real particularity (and capable of only ersatz particularity grasped at defensively over against others) and of real universality (and capable of only abstract universality as the rhetoric of rights or denunciations). The doctrine of original sin, rather than being the abstract declaration of the universal equality in sin of all human beings, is the doctrine of the incapacity for equality outside the ecclesial hypostasis. This can be seen even in the most basic existential terms. It is life in the ecclesial communion that enables persons to discover, to their relief, and relax into their similarity with others.[27]

---

27. Alison, *Joy of Being Wrong*, 181. This quote comes from a section of this chapter called, "Excursus: The Particular Overcoming of Particularity."

I take the implications of this to be quite simple. The reason that Christian and non-Christian find ourselves dominated by our "concern for health" is because medicine in the absence of the church cannot help but dominate our lives. For medicine has become a powerful practice without end, without context, without any wider community to give it purpose. Accordingly nothing could be more important today than for Christians to recover a Christian practice of medicine shaped by the practices of the church, and in particular, baptism. For as Alison observes, it is through baptism that we are introduced to undistorting desire through the pacific imitation of Christ. That this is not a voluntaristic exercise is clear from the fact that the exorcisms, which free us from Satan's kingdom, are celebrated as intrinsic to baptism. Thus through baptism we are simultaneously incorporated into the church and our sins are forgiven. For as Alison observes, incorporation into the church and the forgiveness of sins become the same reality: induction into eternal life.[28] For lives determined by that reality — that is, the reality of life with God — how sickness is understood and cared for cannot help but look quite different than how the world understands what it means to be sick.[29]

---

28. Alison, *Joy of Being Wrong*, 184.

29. Of course, this does not mean there will not be similarities between how Christians and non-Christians understand as well as care for the sick. But what appears as a "sickness" in the world (i.e., growing old) cannot be so understood by Christians. Nor can Christians invest the power in medicine "to relieve the human estate" so characteristic of modern medicine.

Necessarium Adae Peccatum: The Problem of Original Sin

GARY A. ANDERSON

The story of Adam and Eve's transgression, though surprisingly brief, did not prevent subsequent interpreters from pouring enormous attention upon it. The great English Puritan and poet John Milton expanded the several dozen verses of this story into his epic poem, *Paradise Lost,* a work comprised of twelve books, with each book containing nearly a thousand lines. Moderns are frequently wont to characterize such expansions of the biblical original as classic examples of *eisogesis* (reading into the text what one expects to find). The label is not inaccurate, but neither is it particularly apt. To understand even a few lines of a work like *Paradise Lost,* or nearly any other Jewish or Christian elaboration, one must bear in mind another theological and deeply scriptural principle. *The story of human beginnings is only intelligible in light of its end.* In other words, like any good novel, short story, or play, the first scene almost invariably hints, in some way, at how the story will unfold. Upon completing a story, a good reader will return to the opening to see how the end illuminates the beginning.

Much of Milton's expansion of the story of Adam and Eve is dependent on the exegetical principle that the end will illuminate the beginning. Consider what happens when Adam transgresses the interdiction regarding the tree of knowledge:

Earth Trembled from her entrails as again
In pangs, and nature gave a second groan,

22

> Sky loured and muttering thunder, some sad drops
> Wept at completing of the mortal sin
> Original. (*Paradise Lost*, IX: 1000-1004)

These remarkable lines surprise. Where in Genesis 3 do we see signs of cosmic disturbance in the wake of Adam's sin? Has Milton used his poetic license to embellish the terse original? Hardly. These depictions of nature's groaning point forward to nature's travail at Golgotha. As Christ, the creator of the world, hangs on the cross, the earth quakes, the skies darken. So shocking is this sight that one anonymous homilist from the fifth century wrote: "Not even the sun was able to endure this sight but completely darkened itself to block the eyes of others. Neither did it take thought of the commandment to give light (Gen. 1:16) but from that moment on dared to transgress it, seeing the Lord, the giver of commandment, suffering at the hands of man."[1] But there is no reason to be shamed by this sight, our patristic homilist argues, "for if we see the reason for which the Lord suffered, we no longer blush but stand in awe before his goodness and love for mankind." Milton's depiction of the cosmic disturbances that attended Adam's sin orients the reader to the larger drama of Christian redemption.

And so it was for every Jewish and Christian reader of the Bible. The most important matter for their interpretations of Genesis was an awareness of where the story reached its climax.[2] Though this procedure may sound rather simple, in practice it was not. Christian and Jewish perceptions of the story of man's beginnings differ widely. This is because each tradition has a very different idea about what the "end" of the biblical story is.

---

1. "Homily on the Passion of Our Lord," falsely attributed to St. Athanasius, *PG* 28.204.

2. On the importance of knowing the full narrative horizon of the scriptural story see the essay of Robert Jensen, "How the World Lost its Story," *First Things* 36 (1993): 19-24. His remarks on the poetics of Aristotle are particularly relevant: "[T]he sequential events [of any realistic narrative like the Bible] are understood jointly to make a certain kind of sense — a dramatic kind of sense. Aristotle provided the classic specification of dramatically coherent narrative. In a dramatically good story, he said, each decisive event is unpredictable until it happens, but immediately upon taking place is seen to be exactly what "had" to happen. So, to take the example of Aristotle's own favorite good story, we could not know in advance that Oedipus would blind himself but once he has done it instantly see that the whole story must lead to and flow from just this act."

The Beginning in Light of the End

According to the Bible, the sin of Adam and Eve and all that it engendered (banishment from Eden, toiling upon the land, suffering in childbirth, and the return to the soil at death) was a first stage in a progression of general human rebellion. After the Fall we read of Cain's slaying of Abel, the strange tale of the intercourse between the "sons of God and the daughters of men," the various evils that led to the flood, and finally the building of the tower of Babel. Humanity was progressively alienating itself from its divine Creator. This escalating fall from grace took a dramatic turn toward restoration when God appeared before Abraham and promised:

> Go from your country and your kindred and your father's house to the land that I will show you. I will make you a great nation and I will bless you, and make your name great, so that you will be a blessing. . . . Through you all the families of the earth shall bless themselves. (Gen. 12:1-3)

Because the land promised to Abraham was thought of in near-Edenic terms ("a land flowing with milk and honey"), the possession of that land by a specially favored nation was thought to constitute a fitting redress to the fall. At first, the selection of Abraham, the progenitor of Israel, appears to be an improbable way to restore mankind. This special address, directed to one man from amid the many nations, could be seen as unmotivated, unnatural, and even unfair. Yet the mystery of this choice seems to be part of the intention of the author. As Gerhard von Rad observed: "The narrator does not explain why God's choice did not fall upon Ham or Japheth, but rather upon Shem, and [. . .] upon Abraham."[3] This act of unmotivated choice is most often labeled the mystery (or even, the scandal) of election; God has chosen to redeem the entirety of creation through the agency of a single nation. The nation that is imagined by this promise is not simply Israel, but the grand kingdom of Israel realized in the days of Kings David and Solomon. For during their reigns, the borders of the biblical kingdom had an enormous reach, they encroached on the greatest nations of the ancient world.

Gerhard von Rad identified the author of this promise to Abraham

3. Gerhard von Rad, *Genesis* (Philadelphia: Westminster, 1961), 159.

as the "J" or Yahwistic-source, a writer who lived during the grand days of the Davidic kingdom. In his view, the achievements of this kingdom constituted a fulfillment of the promise made to Abraham and hence, a redress of the imbalance wrought by the fall. This hypothetical reconstruction of the narrative history of the Bible has persuaded many, but by no means all biblical scholars. Even if we grant von Rad his hypothesis, it is nevertheless true that for most of the biblical period, specifically the many years that followed the reigns of David and Solomon, the promise given to Abraham was always viewed as unfulfilled and openended. Through the course of time, biblical authors assumed a flexible posture toward this promise. No subsequent biblical or later Jewish author felt constrained or hemmed in by the specific intention of the text's author. For the Yahwistic writer had penned this text in a very broad and generic fashion. As a result it possessed an enormous temporal reach: it extended to the most distant of futures, the consummation of human history. In the words of von Rad this text "refused any [singular and detailed] description of its final end."[4]

If we survey the broadest outline of biblical history we will see that the fulfillment of the promise to Abraham reached an initial apogee with the deliverance of Israel from the hand of Pharaoh and the gift of the Bible or "Torah" to Moses at Mount Sinai. At that moment in time, Israel was formally adopted as God's firstborn or favored son. This moment of election and law-giving was meant to culminate in the taking of the promised land, the very heart of the promise made to Abraham. The gift of the land, however, was never fully realized. From the very first moment, when Moses commissioned spies to reconnoiter the boundaries of Canaan, the taking of the land was beset with problems. During the reigns of David and Solomon, Israel came the closest to realizing the grandeur of the promise, but her moment of glory was ever so brief. Eventually Israel lost the land they occupied when the Babylonian armies invaded. Ever since, Israel has awaited the final ingathering of those who were dispersed, the rebuilding of the temple, and a renewed commitment by the entire nation to return with repentant hearts to the Torah.

As the hope of realizing the promise slipped further and further into the future, the end itself, as Paul Ricœur notes, changed in meaning. And as the tale of Israel's "end" changed so did her beginning:

4. von Rad, *Genesis*, 160.

The fulfillment of the Promise [to Abraham] which at first appears to be at hand, is constantly postponed. In the meantime, the revelation at Sinai, the knowledge of the Law, the setting up of a cult, and the experience in the wilderness take place. The wealth of the interval is such that the end itself changes its meaning. . . . Henceforth the "Promise" will express its tension through the mythical images of the end; those images and the figures in which they will be crystallized will supply the true answer to the images and figures of the beginning.[5]

In the time of Jesus, when Rabbinic Judaism was taking root in Palestine, Judaism was slowly transforming itself from a religion whose "end" or central purpose centered around a temple and sacrifice to a religion focused on prayer and Torah study. According to the Rabbis, Moses received two Torahs at Mount Sinai, one written on tablets, the other transmitted orally. It was the duty of all subsequent generations to pass on this legacy of a twofold Torah and to bring the Jewish nation to a position of faithful obedience of its norms. It would be difficult to find a Jewish writer from this time period who did not draw careful comparisons between the creation of man and the gift of the Torah. In the mind of the Rabbis, God himself consulted the Torah in order to create man and the world he was to inhabit. The end of man's existence, obedience to Torah, was correlated to his very origins.

Christian writers do not take a similar interest in Torah. The writings of St. Paul and the results of the first ecclesial council in Jerusalem (Acts 15) show us that at a very early date, the nascent Christian movement decided to part company with their Jewish brethren over certain aspects of Jewish law. This was because Paul, and others like him, felt that the resurrection of Christ had ushered in a new epoch in human history. This new epoch had no need for the ceremonial details of the Jewish law code, namely those that dealt with sacrifice, bodily purity, and food laws. The goal of human creation was no longer thought to be the giving of the Torah to Israel but the birth, life, and death of Jesus Christ.

It has frequently been noted that Jesus himself made no mention of the story of Adam and Eve in any of the four canonical Gospels. Though he dealt with topics of human sin, the need for repentance, and the promise of salvation for the entire created order, he never

5. Paul Ricœur, *The Symbolism of Evil* (New York: Harper and Row, 1967), 263.

once elucidated the story of Eden in the course of his teaching. This should not be overly surprising. For it is a basic feature of each Gospel that Jesus' true identity, and hence the purpose of the incarnation itself, was not known until after his death. The Gospel of Mark is perhaps the most radical on this point; only the Roman centurion standing at the foot of the cross would figure out who Jesus was when he exclaimed, "Truly this man was God's son!" (15:39). To be sure, the other disciples, especially Peter, would, on occasion identify Jesus as the Christ. But the disciples believed that this Messianic office precluded any tinge of ignominy. Jesus, they thought, was to fill this office in a glorious manner. The moment Jesus alluded to the necessity of his suffering, the disciples rebuked him severely. Only at the resurrection did the disciples finally come to understand the nature of Jesus' identity. In other words, the particular goal or "end" toward which Jesus moved was not made clear until after he had died. Only after his death could the purpose or "end" of Christ's life be joined to the narrative of human beginnings.

The very first Christian document to make this connection was St. Paul's letter to the Corinthians. This letter can be dated to within a couple of decades after the death of Christ (56 or 57 A.D.), not too long after Paul's own conversion to the movement. In the fifteenth chapter he takes up the problem of certain members of the community who lack a clear conviction about the bodily resurrection of Christ. Paul begins his argument by acknowledging that his own teaching is simply a handing on of what he had received. Christ, Paul declares, was buried and "rose on the third day in accordance with the scriptures. He appeared to Cephas then to the twelve. Then he appeared to more than five hundred brothers and sisters at one time. . . . Then he appeared to James, then to all the apostles, last of all, as to one untimely born, he appeared also to me" (1 Cor. 15:4-8). From this brief resume we can see that Paul has established the facticity of Christ's resurrection on evidence greater than his own personal authority. The teaching is founded on a tradition for which Paul is merely a conduit, and, more importantly, Jesus' appearance is an event whose witnesses number in the hundreds.

Paul's interest is not to establish merely the truth of the resurrection. Taken on its own, the event of Jesus' bodily resurrection would seem a wondrous miracle that befell one particular person. For Paul, the event was epoch-making and had cosmic significance. In order to underscore the universal dimensions of this event, Paul introduced the figure of Adam (1 Cor. 15:20-23):

> But in fact Christ has been raised from the dead, the first fruits of those who have died. But since death came through a human being, the resurrection of the dead has come through a human being; for as all die in Adam, so all will be made alive in Christ. But each in his own order: Christ the first fruits, then at his coming those who belong to Christ.

Paul was aware, as any Jewish reader of the Bible would be, that Adam was the personal name of a literary figure in Genesis but also a noun designating mankind more generally. What happened to Adam in Genesis 2–3 was not limited to him alone; by virtue of his name ("mankind") it had ramifications for all persons. If the first *(protos)* Adam died, Paul reasoned, then all must die through him. Since Christ was the second or final *(eschatos)* Adam, his death and resurrection must have had universal dimensions. The resurrection was not an isolated or singular event in world history for it did not involve one man alone but all mankind.

Paul brings this argument home by considering the character of the resurrection body (1 Cor. 15:42-49):

> So it is with the resurrection of the dead. What is sown is perishable, what is raised is imperishable. It is sown in dishonor, it is raised in glory. It is sown in weakness, it is raised in power. It is sown a physical body, it is raised a spiritual body. If there is a physical body there is also a spiritual body. Thus it is written, "the first [*protos*] man, Adam, became a living being" [Gen. 2:7]; the last [*eschatos*] Adam became a life-giving spirit. But it is not the spiritual that is first, but the physical, and then the spiritual. The first man was from the earth, a man of dust; the second man is from heaven. As was the man of dust, so are those who are of the dust; and as is the man of heaven, so are those who are of heaven. Just as we have borne the image [*eikon*] of the man of dust, so we will also bear the image of the man of heaven.

What is striking about this argument is that Paul believes that two epochs characterize the growth of human history, the age of the first and of the second Adam. From the first Adam, a being created from the dust, came a frail and corruptible body; from the second Adam, a life-giving spirit. Those who have faith in the second Adam "bear the image of the man of heaven." It should be carefully noted that Paul begins his argument about the significance of Adam with the fact of Christ's resurrection. It is the last Adam who sets the stage for an understanding of the first.

Lest one think that only Christians understood the beginning in terms of the end, it is worth attending to a Jewish text written in an era roughly contemporary to that of Paul. The book of *4 Ezra* is a document written shortly after the destruction of Jerusalem in 70 A.D. Although this book was written by a Jew for a Jewish audience, it was not included within the Rabbinic Bible. We owe the happy fact of the book's preservation to the early church. But this should not obscure the fact that this book is an important witness to Jewish thinking in the first century about the problem of theodicy, that is, why God inflicts such unmerited suffering on his chosen people. Many have seen in this book a striking parallel to Paul's notion of original sin. In his most despairing moment, the author of *4 Ezra* complains that human life is simply not worth enduring given the painful legacy of sin and death that Adam has bequeathed to us (7:116-117):

> This is my first and last comment: it would have been better if the earth had not produced Adam, or else, when it had produced him, had restrained him from sinning. For what good is it to all that they live in sorrow now and expect punishment after death? O Adam, what have you done? For though it was you who sinned, the fall was not yours alone, but ours also who are your descendants.

One is tempted to interpret these lines as bearing on a *general* proclivity of the human race toward sinfulness. The earth produced Adam, and Adam in turn produced sin and death. These basic features are common to all human life. But to understand the text this broadly would not fit the context of the book. The writer wants to know why *the elected nation of Israel* has suffered so grievously for her sins. Why has she, of all nations, lost her Temple and national capital?

As pessimistic as this description of Adam's legacy may sound, it must not be isolated from the larger picture of what the Jewish Bible is all about. In an earlier portion of *4 Ezra*, the author retells the story of the six days of creation. When he arrives on the sixth day, the day of man's creation, he writes (6:53-54):

> On the sixth day you commanded the earth to bring forth before you
> cattle, wild animals, and creeping things; and over these you placed
> Adam, as ruler over all the works that you had made; and from him
> we have all come, the people whom you have chosen.

It is striking that Adam's creation is wed to the notion of Israel's special status in God's eyes. *In Ezra's view, the creation of Adam in the image
of God points forward to the election of Israel.*

The problem can be brought into bolder relief. The issue is not
simply that of why do the good suffer, but why does Israel in particular — that nation which represents the very pinnacle of human creation — suffer worse than all the rest of humanity (6:55-59):

> All this I have spoken before you, O Lord, because you have said that
> it was for us that you created this world. As for the other nations that
> have descended from Adam, you have said that they are nothing, and
> that they are like spittle and you have compared their abundance to a
> drop from a bucket. And now, O Lord, these nations which are re-
> puted to be as nothing, dominate over us and devour us. But we are
> your people, whom you have called your firstborn, only begotten,
> zealous for you, and most dear, have been given into their hands. If
> the world has indeed been created for us, why do we not possess our
> world as an inheritance? How long will this be so?

The imagery used to depict Israel is striking. The elected nation is
understood as God's "firstborn" and "only begotten"; these are precisely the same titles used by Paul and other New Testament writers
to describe Christ.[6] This similar choice of words allows us to draw a
close parallel between Paul and 4 Ezra. As Paul saw creation culminate in the figure of the second Adam and drew his picture of the
first Adam as an antitype to him, so *4 Ezra* saw the figure of Adam
culminate in the choosing of the people Israel. The nub of Ezra's
problem is the fact that the nations have risen up and usurped the
rightful position of glory that should belong to the nation Israel.
Why have those who have descended from Adam overtaken those
who claim their origins at Sinai? For *4 Ezra*, the story of Adam's creation and its bearing on world history cannot be understood apart

6. On the terms "first-born" and "only begotten" and their relationship to the
theme of election, see the comments of Michael Stone, *Fourth Ezra,* Hermeneia (Minneapolis: Fortress Press, 1990), 188-189.

from the act of God's decision to give Israel the Torah at Mt. Sinai. The Bible's beginning must be correlated with its end. Strikingly, very few modern biblical scholars consider this history of religions' concept a necessary part of Genesis 1–3. As a result, it should occasion no surprise if the doctrine of original sin has fallen upon hard times.

The Problem of Original Sin

For many today the most pressing problem created by an emphasis on Adam's sin is that it implies a low estimation of the human person. How can human nature improve and flower if it is defined from the very start as wayward, recalcitrant, and worthy of death? In our modern secular age, an age in which the continued existence of religion itself is questioned, it is difficult to advance an argument for the inherent sinfulness of each and every human being. Why would any modern man or woman define their essential humanity in terms of a transgression committed by a primal couple whose very historical existence they do not believe? If the fossil record has made the historical existence of Adam and Eve improbable, why should we accept the conclusion that their sin continues to hound and even damn us? It is little wonder that the doctrine of original sin has fallen on such hard times. As one astute observer, Edward Oakes, has observed,

> No doctrine inside the precincts of the Christian Church is received with greater reserve and hesitation, even to the point of outright denial, than the doctrine of original sin. Of course in a secular culture like ours, any number of Christian doctrines will be disputed by outsiders, from the existence of God to the resurrection of Jesus. But even in those denominations that pride themselves on their adherence to the orthodox dogmas of the once-universal Church, the doctrine of original sin is met with either embarrassed silence, outright denial, or at a minimum a kind of halfhearted lip service that does not exactly deny the doctrine but has no idea how to place it inside the devout life.[7]

7. Edward Oakes, "Original Sin: A Disputation," *First Things* 87 (1998): 16. Much of this section of my essay has been inspired by this excellent article.

The doctrine of original sin appears woefully ill-matched to modern existence. This teaching outlines our common human condition in such stark and grim terms that it no longer inspires. Indeed, the effect is far worse. Its pervasive pessimistic outlook leaves little room for contemplating our vast potential for grandeur. In the eyes of many, the task of successfully navigating the turbulent seas of the late twentieth century demands that we jettison this burdensome cargo in favor of more affirming and joyful views.

The writings of the former Benedictine priest, Matthew Fox, provide a good barometer of how strong this cultural suspicion is. Angered by the recalcitrance of current religious thinkers to reconsider past truisms about the fall of man, he outlined his own proposal in a book titled, *Original Blessing*.[8] Fox argues that the concept of original sin is rooted in an incorrigible attitude of self-loathing. When the church demands that we ponder deeply our own wretched state, we not only make ourselves miserable, but we undermine our sense of connection and integration with the larger created order. For it is from this very sense of connection and integration, Fox argues, that our civic responsibilities grow. Absent these delicate roots that bind us to each other and to our planet, there is no telling what evils will surface in their place.

Fox's solution seems a sensible one. Replace the difficult and irreformable notion of human depravity with a different story of our origins. The Bible itself, Fox argues, presents its own competing view of the created order, a view of a more optimistic tenor. In the so-called wisdom traditions of the Old Testament, we are beckoned to become disciples of Lady Wisdom and give heed to her kind teaching. Lady Wisdom appears in the book of Proverbs as the very artisan of creation. *"When God marked out the foundations of the earth,"* Lady Wisdom reveals (Prov. 8:29b-31), *"I was there beside him, like a master worker. I was daily his delight, rejoicing before him always, rejoicing in his inhabited world and delighting in the human race."* Lady Wisdom gives no thought to human depravity; her expectations for human life are of a different order. No preacher of fire and damnation, her pedagogy assumes a kinder, gentler air. She built her home, set her table, prepared a feast, and then sought students (9:5): *"Come, eat of my bread, and drink of the*

8. Matthew Fox, *Original Blessing: A Primer in Creation Spirituality in Four Paths, Twenty-Six Themes, and Two Questions* (Santa Fe: Bear Press, 1983).

wine I have mixed. Lay aside immature thoughts and truly live, walk in the way of insight."

For Fox, the way of wisdom is the way of mother earth. Wisdom affirms our world as good and blessed and seeks to establish us as responsible stewards over this created order. Reflection on this order through the tutelage of Lady Wisdom will result in human wholeness. Human proclivities to destroy our planet will be checked; the potential for intercultural dialogue and understanding will be realized. An affirming, feminine God who reveals to us our most profound potential replaces the menacing patriarchal God who laid the notion of depravity at the doorstep of all.

Unfortunately, much of Fox's argument depends on a very narrow slice of biblical teaching about Lady Wisdom. His euphoria over those points of overlap between this ancient biblical theme and his very modern, New Age spiritual predilections, blinds him to some of the darker aspects of Wisdom in the Bible. The book of Job, for example, certainly the Bible's most profound exploration of the nature and consequence of evil, is not at all optimistic about Wisdom's capacity to lay bare the fundaments of our created world. Has God ordered his creation so that those who act rightly will be rewarded? Job's friends present the expected answer — yes! — and are subsequently rebuked. For Job the matter is far from clear. Innocence need not be rewarded; evil is frequently left unpunished. *"Where can Wisdom be found,"* Job cries (ch. 28). The answer is not one of reassurance: *"It is hidden from the eyes of all living, and concealed from the birds of the air."* Not even the dead have a privileged point of access. *"We have heard,"* Death and Hell confess, *"only a rumor of it with our ears."* Wisdom, in any full sense of the term, is in God's hands alone. Don't be too hasty in your desire to define Wisdom's scope, another Wisdom writer warns: *"God is in heaven and you are on earth; therefore let your words be few"* (Eccles. 5:2).

Even if we reject Fox's overly buoyant hopes for a creation-centered spirituality, we still have not countered his stinging criticism of original sin. Even more challenging is the seconding of Fox's criticisms by other scholars whose intellectual preferences do not rest on the moral platitudes of New Age spirituality. Consider the Requiems written by Fauré and Duruflé in our own time. Both of these composers left out the haunting words of God's harsh judgment on the unjust, the *Dies Irae*. Both composers had a strong distaste for the punitive words of God at the moment of death; far better in their eyes was a funeral mass that laid sole emphasis on the merciful hand of God. Or consider the noted and notable Presbyterian biblical scholar, Sibley Towner.[9] He begins his essay with the formulation of original sin that appears in the *Scots Confession of 1560*. This was not an insignificant document; indeed it was publicly read line by line in the Scottish Parliament. This confession of faith declares that by Adam's "transgression, generally known as original sin, . . . he and his children became by nature hostile to God, slaves of Satan and servants to sin." However powerful such a declaration might have been in its own day, Towner claims that it has also "wrought incalculable mischief in the hearts of believers."[10] The failure of the doctrine of original sin does not simply rest in depressive ambiance about human nature that it has produced. Its very claim as historical fact is simply preposterous. "Modern believers and unbelievers alike tend to hold as patent nonsense the notion that all human sin and all death are generically descended from a single act by a single pair of human beings who lived at a single moment in time, or that the cause of their original transgression was Satan in the guise of a snake."[11]

What are we to make of such a doctrine? Towner's answer is simple and forthright. We must act with the courage of our convictions and seek to move beyond it. "The concept of a Fall-less history," he argues, "requires some further maturation in me away from the religion of my Sunday School and my dogmatics textbooks." This rewriting of Christian tradition will be difficult, Towner concedes, but it will also be a bracing tonic for twentieth-century man, whose self-esteem has suffered the outrageous slings and arrows of narrow dogmatism for too long. "Perhaps I can at last see us," he concludes, "not as creatures helplessly mired in sin, helpless to extricate ourselves in any way, but rather as people and peoples who can hope to make significant strides toward emancipation from the evils of hatred and greed."[12] It would take a real curmudgeon to fault Towner for these laudable desires for emancipation. And I should also add that Towner has adequately described the problems of adhering to Genesis 1–3 as a literal account of

9. Sibley Towner, "Interpretations and Reinterpretations of the Fall," in *Modern Biblical Scholarship: Its Impact on Theology and Proclamation*, ed. Francis A. Eigo (Villanova, PA: Villanova University Press, 1984), 53-85.

10. Cited in Towner, "Interpretations," 56-57.

11. Towner, "Interpretations," 57-58.

12. Towner, "Interpretations," 82.

human beginnings. Modern theologians and biblical scholars are agreed that we must move beyond *historical* literalism. But is Towner accurate regarding what the church confesses *theologically* about *peccatum originale?*

O Necessary Sin . . . O Happy Fault!

A good place to test this notion is the figure of John Milton. Raised on the theological writings of St. Augustine and deeply committed to the rigorous Puritan tradition, Milton is deeply aware of how weak and prone to sin and error the human creature is. The Puritanism of Milton was not far removed from the strain that produced the *Scots Confession of 1560,* a document much abhorred by Sibley Towner and numerous other moderns. If the tradition of original sin is as gloomy as Towner and Fox believe, we would expect Milton's grand epic, *Paradise Lost,* to end on a somber note. Adam's loss of grace and eviction from Eden would be a matter of profound tragic loss and deepest despair. Satan's triumph, on the other hand, should have been a moment of ecstatic delight in the kingdom of darkness. After all, Adam and Eve had proved sufficiently gullible for the most simple of temptations to take fertile root.

In fact, we find nothing of the kind. True, Satan achieved his desire; Adam and Eve fell. Yet Satan's last appearance in *Paradise Lost* is not a happy one. His return to hell is greeted with lamentation, not celebration. His is a pyrrhic victory. Adam and Eve, on the other hand, have lost all that they held dear. Condemned to permanent exile, we would expect their mood to be morose as they leave the garden. Such is not the case. As *Paradise Lost* draws to a close, Adam is exultant as he makes his way out of Eden.

The poem had begun with Satan in the bowels of hell, gathering his compatriots in crime and rebellion to embark on the task of alienating God from his beloved creatures, Adam and Eve. Through some nine books, each nearly a thousand verses, we follow his peregrinations from hell to earth and then back to hell. On the surface, Satan has the best of it. His power to tempt Eve proves insurmountable. Despite all God's precautions — and there were many — the creatures he loved so dearly rebel against His rule. The reader has every right to expect that as Satan rejoins his comrades in Pandemonium, Milton's name for hell, all will rejoice. Milton subverts this expectation. As Satan enters Pandemonium, he recounts the circumstances of his mighty triumph and closes with these words (X:501-503):

> "Ye have the account
> Of my performance: what remains, ye gods,
> But up and enter now into full bliss."

But his cohorts see no cause for celebration. Instead of cries of joy Satan hears,

> A dismal universal hiss, the sound
> Of public scorn.

The mood turns even more mordant as these unlikely celebrants consider their present state. In hopes of alleviating their aching pains the demonic host turns to consider the fair fruits of hell. These fruits appear enticing; perhaps they would be a balm for their ills. As the demons reach for this "fruitage fair" an unexpected result ensues (X:564-566),

> Thinking to allay
> Their appetite with gust, instead of fruit
> Chewed bitter ashes.

In a surprising parallel to the fall of Adam and Eve, the fruits of Hades prove deceptive. When the demons chew its bitter ashes they undergo the first stage of that ancient curse pronounced on the serpent, "you shall eat the dust of the earth."

This is our last glimpse of Satan in *Paradise Lost*. The fall, which should have been his moment of glory, has confirmed his eternal condemnation.

Our last glimpse of Milton's Adam is also quite striking. The archangel Michael stands with Adam and Eve at the edge of Eden. Just prior to driving them out he briefs Adam on what life outside will be like. Michael outlines the entire biblical story beginning with their own children, Cain and Abel. When Michael finishes describing the life of Christ, he pauses to catch his breath. Adam cannot endure the pause, however brief. He loses his composure as he hears these mysteries. He exclaims (XII:469-471):

> "O Goodness infinite, goodness immense!
> That all this good of evil shall produce,
> And evil turn to good."

But Adam doesn't stop here. Not only will his evil deed be turned to good, but it shall also become the necessary prelude for the appearance of a far greater good.

Milton's brilliant and surprising ending is not solely the work of his own poetic genius. His narrative is dependent upon a theological tradition that viewed Adam's sin as a true boon for mankind. This notion of the *felix culpa*, or "happy fault," has a long pedigree in Christian thought. An ancient liturgy of Easter opens with a hymn reciting God's mighty deeds in history, the *Exultet*. This hymn compares the Israelite's exodus from Egypt to the resurrection of Christ. On that first paschal night, the slaying of the Passover lamb proved instrumental in overturning the tyranny of Pharaoh; on this second paschal occasion, the sacrifice of the Lamb of God will destroy a second Pharaoh, Satan and his kingdom. In consideration of the great redemption that Christ has wrought, the cantor sings of Adam's sin. In the wake of the long period of Lenten penance that had preceded Easter, a time in which all Christians must ponder their sinful ways, the memory of Adam's transgression should stir up thoughts of condemnation. But the text of the *Exultet* knows no such thought. In words that delight as much as they shock, the cantor sings,

> "O *necessary* sin of Adam, that Christ has blotted out by his death;
> O *happy* fault (*felix culpa*) which has earned for us such a great
> redeemer."

How unexpected are these words. But their strangeness reveals the central mystery of Easter: the human capacity for rebellion has not led to eternal condemnation but to the miracle of God's loving and steadfast mercy.

Milton understood well the theology of "the happy fault" and makes it the basis of Adam's own self-reflection after the fall. To the surprise of many readers, Adam cannot decide whether he should repent of his sin or rejoice all the more. His sin has provided the necessary condition for making God's boundless mercy manifest. Adam declares (XII:473-478),

"Full of doubt I stand,
Whether I should repent me now of sin
By me done and occasioned, or rejoice
Much more good thereof shall spring
to God more glory, more good will to men
From God, and over wrath grace shall abound."

Our present-day "cultured despisers" of original sin do not lack good
reason when they criticize this doctrine in its raw and naked form. I
sincerely doubt whether Milton or the composer of the *Exultet* would
have warmed to the assertion that our nature is corrupt to the core
and that we merit nothing less than unending punishment and damnation. Such a view advanced too stridently would veer toward the
blasphemous. When these writers condemn Adam, and through
Adam all humanity, they do so in the context of a larger narrative that
exalts him. Adam's humiliation leads ineluctably to his exaltation.
This is the paradox of original sin, a paradox that has been little no-
ticed in our day.

Original Sin and Redemption

Original sin is not a self-contained philosophical doctrine, but depends on the religious experience of redemption. The moment we isolate the sin of Adam from this broader framework we lose its larger
meaning. One of the most profound thinkers of the twentieth century,
Karl Barth, devoted considerable energy toward recovering what
Christian thought meant by the doctrine of original sin. Barth was
raised on the liberal theology standard in German theological education at the close of the nineteenth century and the beginning of the
twentieth. The optimism regarding the human condition that had
been a formative part of that tradition was brutally undercut, Barth
thought, by the tragedy of the First World War. His turn to the Bible
as a source of inspiration for theological work was born, in part, from
a deep distrust of what he felt was an overly optimistic assessment of
what philosophical knowledge could and would yield. One might have
expected Barth to begin his work by returning to the classic Protestant
teachings on original sin.

But this was not what he did. Instead, when Barth sat down to write his greatest theological work, *Church Dogmatics,* he did not take up the topic of original sin until the end of the work. And this was not accidental. As he wrote:

> But the question immediately poses itself: Why is it only now that we have come to speak of this matter? Why have we not followed the example of the dogmatics of all ages, Churches and movements and begun with a doctrine of sin, first stating the problem, then giving the decisive answer to it in the doctrine of the incarnation and atoning death of Jesus Christ?[13]

Traditional Protestant teaching had attempted to erect the edifice of Christian belief on an objective portrayal of human depravity. Deep reflection on one's depravity was thought to be one short step from perceiving one's need for a redeemer. For Barth, this argument was foolish on two grounds. First, if all human beings were so depraved, one could just as easily rationalize one's own evil in a self-serving way: "My actions may be despicable, but they are no worse than anyone else's. My sinful state is simply a part of the general human condition." Far from impelling the individual into the arms of a merciful redeemer, such a doctrine could just as easily serve to comfort sinful persons in their wrongdoing.

Barth had another, more biblical manner of getting at this question. He argued that no one could understand his status as "a lowly sinner" apart from the miracle of redemption. "We can never have the negative knowledge [of sin]," Barth declared, "except in [light of] this positive faith."[14] Barth fervently denied the capacity of any person to understand his fallen condition by contemplating his wayward ways. We may become aware of our limited and deficient nature by doing so. We may even incline toward despair and hopelessness. But this is not what the Bible means by sin. The fathomless depth of sin can only be glimpsed under the tutelage of the Redeemer. The experience of redemption, in Barth's eyes, was always that of an unmerited *bonum,* or gift, to the believer. Not asked for and not deserved, redemption always comes as an unexpected act of Grace. *The notion of human sin and fallenness is nothing other than a considered reflection on the unmerited and unfathomable moment of salvation.*

13. Karl Barth, *Church Dogmatics* (Edinburgh: T & T Clark, 1957), IV, 359.
14. Barth, *Church Dogmatics,* IV, 413.

Barth's claim about the love of God can be paralleled in our own deepest attachments. Nearly any romantic tale worth its salt will accent the profound power of love by showing its ability to transform both the lover and the beloved. Yet the power and the strength of that love nearly always is established on the fragile and frail foundation of human nature. The attitude of the beloved is never one of merit or entitledness: "I had this coming," but precisely the opposite: "I don't deserve this." As the poets are well aware, the beloved never feels worthy of the advances of the lover. When Jewish or Christian mystics appeal to their divine lover to "draw me after you, let us make haste [to your bed-chamber]" (Song of Songs 1:4) they utter these words in awe. True love is unmerited love.

In a profound way, the same process informs the teaching of original sin. In the religious life, human sinfulness can only be grasped as a reflection on the unmerited advances of the divine lover toward his beloved. When the church prays, "Let him kiss me with the kisses of his mouth" (Song of Songs 1:2), she is directing her erotic desire toward the advances of her divine lover. Yet the erotic appeal of the church to her divine lover is born from the consciousness of her own unworthiness of that love.

In a similar fashion, consider the gospel reading that introduces the period of Lenten penance in both the Eastern and Western liturgies. It is, quite ironically, the story of the prodigal son (Luke 15:11-32). The prodigal son is a young man who received an inheritance that he subsequently squandered through a life of luxury and abandon in a foreign land. Coming to his senses, he sets out for home in order to redress his ways. Arriving at home, he begs for mercy and his father is overcome with joy. His expectations, born of his penitential demeanor, are minimal. "I will get up and go to my father," the son exclaims, "and I will say to him, 'Father, I have sinned against heaven and before you; I am no longer worthy to be called your son; treat me like one of your hired hands" (Luke 15:18-19). The other son, who never exhibited such rebellious behavior, is angered by the festivities that attend his brother's homecoming. "Listen!" he says to his father, "For all these years I have been working like a slave for you, and I have never disobeyed your command; yet you have never given me even a young goat so that I might celebrate with my friends." No doubt, this upright brother had every right to be jealous. But the gospel reading requires this motif of unfairness to make a point: nowhere is there more joy and thanksgiving than when a wayward person rights his course. The gospel narrative brings home, in a powerful way, that the depth of human sin is seen most clearly from the vantage point of one shown mercy. The prodigal son felt himself unworthy of being treated as a son, but his merciful and loving father saw the matter differently. His father did not see a rebellious, wayward son; he saw a son who had once been dead come to life, a son who had been lost but now was found. The unfair reception of the prodigal son serves a profound theological point: the lower one falls, the greater the joy at one's return. Or to reverse the matter, the more powerful one's sense of redemption the more profound is one's sense of sinfulness. As the church enters the Lenten period, the context against which Adam's sin is considered is that of the prodigal son. We are all, in some sense, wayward sons making our way back to a merciful father. The promise of Easter is that the power of sin and redemption are inversely related.

Elsewhere in the Bible we find a similar tendency to correlate human unworthiness with divine grace and mercy. In the Old Testament, the crowning achievement of God's created order is the election of the people Israel at Mt. Sinai and the pronouncement of the Ten Commandments. These Ten Commandments, the first of the six hundred and thirteen to be revealed at Sinai according to Jewish tradition, are heard directly by the people Israel. So awed are they by this encounter that the people become afraid and tremble. Standing at a distance, they beg Moses to intercede on their behalf. For mere mortals to witness the stark purity and overpowering holiness of the Deity was a reckless venture. Who could behold the living God and not die? Aware of their waywardness, they appealed to Moses to approach God on their behalf.

> So now why should we [Israel] die? For this great fire will consume us; if we hear the voice of the Lord our God any longer, we shall die. For who is there of all flesh that has heard the voice of the living God speaking out of fire, as we have, and remained alive? Go near, you yourself [Moses], and hear all that the Lord our God will say. Then tell us everything that the Lord our God tells you, and we will listen and do it. (Deut. 5:25-27)

Everywhere in the Bible when God appears before his people in order to save them, he strikes fear in the hearts of those so blessed. The experience of the divine calls one to reflect on one's frailty. Isaiah begged leave when he entered the presence of God, "Woe is me! I am lost, for I am a man of unclean lips" (Isa. 6). Other prophets begged similar exemptions when God called them by name. *Those graced by the very presence of God are the very persons who reflect most poignantly on their sinful human condition.*

One of Barth's favorite illustrations of this dilemma is the story of Peter's denial of Christ as told in Luke's Gospel (22:31-34; 54-62). Luke, like the rest of the Gospel writers, presents the messianic office of Jesus of Nazareth as a mystery. This vocation was publicly announced at his baptism. Yet throughout his entire earthly life Jesus was rejected for claiming this identity. Those he was sent to redeem sought to destroy him. Even the eleven faithful disciples deserted him during his last hours and he was left to suffer alone. Christ had predicted the denial of one of his most beloved disciples, Simon also known as Peter. "Simon, Simon," Christ said, "Satan has sought to test you as one winnows grain. I have prayed on your behalf that your faith not fail. But you, when you have turned back, strengthen your brothers." Then Peter, acting with a sincerity that is as touching as it is human, counters this prediction with a foolhardy vow, "Lord, I am ready to go with you to prison and to death!" Jesus replies, "I tell you, Peter, the cock will not crow this day until you have denied me three times." Later that evening Jesus is betrayed, arrested, and taken by force to the High Priest's home for interrogation. Peter, following at a distance, enters and takes a seat near an open fire, warming himself outside as Christ is interrogated within. Once, twice, finally a third time, Peter denies ever having known this man from Galilee. As in the other Gospel accounts, the cock crows. Luke's story has not ended. As the cock crows, Jesus looks away from the High Priest and his court that sits ready to condemn him and catches his precious disciple's eye. "Peter remembered the word of the Lord," Luke records, "and he went out and wept bitterly."

Peter's earlier words, although they border on bragging, are hardly contemptible. We err badly if we begrudge him his feeling of confidence. Peter's confidence, whatever its source, runs aground on the shoals of his own fears and self-interest. But his awareness of his failure is contextualized by Luke in the face-to-face encounter with his Lord. As Raymond Brown has remarked: "Jesus had [earlier] prayed for Peter that his faith might not fail, now Jesus is leading his disciple to repentance so that having turned around, he may strengthen others."[15] Peter learns of his sinful predisposition, not as a sterile dogma, nor solely as a moment of hatred and loathing turned inward. His sinful inclination becomes clear only through the loving glance of his Lord, a glance that forgives even as it renders judgment.

Peter's failure is revealed in a face-to-face glance by his redeemer who hastened to forgive even as he issued judgment. And so our paradox: Peter's profound knowledge of this forgiving love, like the knowledge of the prodigal son, springs from a moment of abject failure. The greatness of Peter, which will come to light in the wake of Easter, originated in the weakness he reveals during Jesus' trial.

In the experience of unmerited redemption, the advances of the divine lover seem too grand for words. In the attempt to characterize their awe at this act of God's condescension to humanity, biblical writers give voice to their own sense of inadequacy for such an encounter. It is from precisely this nexus — the merciful approach of God to an unexpectant person — that the notion of original sin takes life. And so Barth's profound insight: original sin is not a reasoned, philosophical consideration of human waywardness and evil, however true these concepts might be on their own terms. The doctrine of original sin is a theological attempt to sketch how profound this mystery and *experience* of redemption truly is.

Adam as Microcosm

To Karl Barth we owe the modern articulation that the depth of human sin can only be known by the redeemed. As the story of Peter's denial of Christ and the parable of the prodigal son illustrate, the locus of human sin is precisely the spot where God's capacity for mercy shines most brilliantly.

Yet one may wonder whether the mercy shown to Peter or the prodigal son are isolated examples or representative of a larger pattern. Would it be more honest to say that the occurrences of love and mercy are distributed randomly across the face of human history? Would the world be better defined as an arbitrary and unjust place?

Christians answer this question with a resounding *No!* For Chris-

15. Raymond Brown, *Death of the Messiah* (New York: Doubleday, 1994), I, 622.

tians, the affirmation that God's mercy defines the very ground of human existence is founded on the basis of Adam's sin and redemption. Just as we could not understand the prodigal son's confession of sin apart from the loving father anxious to forgive and restore him to his place in the family, so we cannot understand Adam's sin without setting it against the backdrop of his redemption. And not by accident, both readings are Lenten texts.

In individual stories of repentance we see the effects of divine mercy in *microcosm;* in the history of Adam this work of redemption is writ large across the *macrocosm.* Any particular moment of tearful confession and redemption is not a random act; it is a participation in the most fundamental structure of the created order. All have died in the first Adam; all will rise through the second. And this is precisely the reason why the Christian tradition has ascribed the fall of man to the sin of just one man. The defeat of that first man is swallowed up by the victory of the last man — Jesus Christ. This is no exercise in literary artistry, as though the writers of the Bible had merely aesthetic interests at stake when they closed this story as it had opened. The purpose was theological. The story ends as it began in order to bring home the point that God's forgiveness of Adam through Christ defines *all* human creation. Individual acts of mercy are not random and episodic; they participate in that grand act of mercy that defines the poles of creation.

Many have claimed that since we can no longer accept the historical existence of Adam and Eve, the story of their sin and redemption can no longer have any meaning. But such a narrow view of how the Bible discloses its meaning misses the entire point. Adam and Eve are significant as individuals not because they represent the very first persons on planet earth, but because they serve the narrative purpose of affirming that all human existence stands under the broad canopy of a merciful God. Forgiveness and grace are not arbitrary moments in the lives of random specimens of the species *homo sapiens.* They are the very center point around which all creation turns — and flourishes. This is the teaching of original sin.

The Eucharist as Sacrament of Union

A. N. WILLIAMS

In a fallen world, one marked by human sin, disorder, and brokenness, and by the manifestation of death and violence in the natural
as well as the human world, how is the presence of God discernible?
One answer is that by faith we see God's victory over sin, wrought
in Christ's death and resurrection, a victory in which we participate
through our incorporation into Christ at baptism. This answer has
the merit of pointing to the once-and-for-all character of our redemption. Baptism, however, cannot be the only Christian answer to sin,
both because the baptized exhibit a disconcerting habit of sinning
with monotonous regularity after their baptism, and because the
New Testament and the practice of the church make provision for
our continuing growth in holiness, the greatest means of which is
the sacrament of the eucharist.

One way of understanding the eucharist's role in proclaiming
Christ's victory over sin and death is to see it as the mechanism
whereby sins are forgiven. This view is grounded in the account of the
Last Supper in the Gospel of St. Matthew, when Jesus gives the cup to
his disciples, saying: "Drink from it, all of you; for this is my blood of
the covenant, which is poured out for many for the forgiveness of
sins" (26:27-28). If the eucharist is to be understood solely, or even
principally, as working forgiveness, however, we must face some difficult problems and questions. First, this stress on the eucharist's pur-

I would like to thank my colleague Bryan Spinks for his helpful critique of an
early draft of this essay.

pose as forgiveness is evident in only one of the Gospel narratives of the Last Supper, that of St. Matthew just cited. Second, the New Testament also ties baptism to the forgiveness of sins; if we assume those receiving the eucharist are baptized, what is the relation between the forgiveness granted in baptism and that granted through the eucharist?[1] More difficult still is the question arising out of eucharistic liturgies in their developed form: If today most begin with some sort of penitential rite, followed by a general confesssion and a formula of either absolution or assurance of pardon, are not those who receive of bread and cup *already* forgiven?[2] Indeed, several churches stipulate that confession and repentance are the prerequisites of receiving communion: in Eastern Orthodox practice, before any communion; in the Roman Catholic, at least when the communicant is in a state of mortal sin. The discipline of Anglican churches provides for the refusal of communion to anyone known by the celebrant to be in a state of serious sin and the traditional exhortation to communion of the 1662 Prayer Book includes a warning to examine oneself and confess, in an auricular confession to a priest if need be, before receiving communion.[3] It is expected by Christians of almost any stripe that communicants will examine themselves carefully before receiving of the bread and cup.

In light of the biblical witness and the practice of the majority of modern Christians, it seems we need a fuller understanding of the relation of the eucharist to sin than simply seeing it as a means of forgiveness. The position I want to develop here is that while the eucharist is integrally related to confession, repentance, and forgiveness, the eucharist itself is today best understood not as forgiving sin, but as perfecting reconciliation by drawing those who receive of bread and

---

1. This relation is explained by Alexander Schmemann, *For the Life of the World: Sacraments and Orthodoxy* (Crestwood, NY: St. Vladimir's, 1988), 78. See also Cyril of Jerusalem, *Lectures on the Christian Sacraments: The Protocatechesis and the Five Mystagogical Catecheses*, ed. F. L. Cross (Crestwood, NY: St. Vladimir's, 1986), II.6, pp. 61-63.

2. Orders for confession and absolution or declaration of pardon are found in the eucharistic rites of the Roman Missal (1969), the Lutheran Book of Worship (1978), the American Book of Common Prayer (1979; all future references to the Book of Common Prayer are to the American Prayer Book, unless noted otherwise), the Methodist Hymnal (1989), and the Book of Common Worship (1993). See Frank C. Senn, *Christian Liturgy: Catholic and Evangelical* (Minneapolis: Fortress Press, 1997), 646-647.

3. See the Book of Common Prayer, pp. 409 and 317 respectively.

wine towards union.[4] It is the grounds for this position and its theological implications to which I now turn.

We begin with the biblical witness. As noted, forgiveness appears as an element of the eucharist in only one of the Gospel accounts of the Last Supper, that of Matthew. The other Synoptics, as
well as Paul's account in 1 Corinthians, stress that the cup is that of
the new covenant. All the Synoptics sound an eschatological note:
Jesus' saying that he will not drink of the vine again until he does so
in the coming kingdom. The Lucan and Pauline texts also underline
remembrance and thanksgiving, while the keynote of the Johannine
discussion of the eucharist (which is not a narrative of the Last Supper itself) is the gift of life that comes through feeding on Christ.
What the New Testament suggests, then, is that the eucharist inau-
gurates and sustains a relation with God that at once looks back to a
past event and forward to a future state. To these temporal associa-
tions may be appropriated our acts of remembrance and thanksgiving and God's act of creating new life in us: remembrance and
thanksgiving to the past, new life to the present and future. That all
of these elements necessarily cohere in a whole is suggested by the
chain of events that the Last Supper begins and the liturgical calen-
dar commemorates as a whole: the Triduum that takes the church
from the memorial of the Last Supper on Maundy Thursday to the
exultation of Easter. In that liturgical cycle, the eucharist leads us
toward the crucifixion *and* the resurrection, just as the Epistles of

4. Schmemann alludes to this idea in *For the Life of the World*, 44. Cf. also Rowan
Williams, *Eucharistic Sacrifice: The Roots of a Metaphor*, Grove Liturgical Studies no. 31
(Bramcote, Notts.: Grove Books, 1982), 32. Geoffrey Wainwright points to the sealing
of reconciliation as one significance of the eucharist for social ethics, see *Doxology:
The Praise of God in Worship, Doctrine and Life* (New York: Oxford University Press,
1980), 431. For a dissenting view, see Ernest Falardeau, *A Holy and Living Sacrifice: Eucharist in Christian Perspective* (Collegeville, MN: Liturgical Press, 1996), 14-23, and
Geoffrey Wainwright, *Eucharist and Eschatology* (London: Epworth, 1971), 89 and 91,
citing Theodore of Mopsuestia, John Damascene, Cyprian, and Ambrose. While the
earliest rites did not begin with penitential orders, their focus was not on what the
eucharist did for the communicant. Geoffrey Grimshaw Willis argues that the earliest
liturgies were sacrifices of praise and so were firmly theocentric; prayers for the fruits
of communion entered liturgies only at the end of the fourth century ("Sacrificium
Laudis" in *The Sacrifice of Praise: Studies in the Theories of Thanksgiving and Redemption in
the Central Prayers of the Eucharistic and Baptismal Liturgies*, ed. Bryan D. Spinks,
Bibliotheca Ephemerides Liturgicae, Subsidia 19 [Rome: Edizioni Liturgiche, 1981],
86-87).

the New Testament tell us that we have both redemption *and* sanctification through Christ's blood (Eph. 1:7; Heb. 13:12).[5] Since the
New Testament affirms that these are linked, but only hints at the
way in which they are related, we will need to examine sacramental
theology and liturgical practice to establish how the eucharist
quenches sin and evil.

Let us begin with the question of the relation of the eucharist to
baptism and confession. The New Testament suggests that one of the
core significations of baptism is as a token, or even means, of repentance (Matt. 3:11 and Acts 2:38); its other purpose seems to be as a
token of membership in Christ and new life in Christ (Matt. 28:19;
Mark 16:16; John 4:1; Acts 19:1-5; Rom. 6:3-4; 1 Cor. 12:13; Gal.
3:27). John the Baptist, however, seems to see a difference between
the baptism he bestows and that of Jesus; his baptism is clearly associated with repentance, while that of Jesus is "with the Holy Spirit"
(Mark 1:4, 8). In the church's understanding, these purposes came to
be joined and elaborated. One of the earliest accounts of the church's
sacramental practice, that of Justin Martyr, describes baptism as a
washing for the remission of sins, whose purpose is regeneration.[6] A
more recent example of such a view is the catechism of the Episcopal
Church, which states: "The inward and spiritual grace in Baptism is
union with Christ in his death and resurrection, birth into God's family the Church, forgiveness of sins, and new life in the Holy Spirit."[7] In
this definition of baptism's effects, the unity of the crucifixion and
resurrection is mirrored in the Christian's own life by the forgiveness
of past sin and the regeneration signified by new birth, new life, and
union with Christ. The new catechism of the Roman Catholic Church
and both Luther's Large and Small Catechisms, while less explicit regarding union, affirm effects that to one degree or another are conso-

---

5. See extracts from the Anglican-Roman Catholic and Lutheran-Roman Catholic
dialogues in Senn, *Christian Liturgy,* 655. The position taken on the eucharist's relation
to forgiveness should not be regarded as either advocating or denying any position vis-
à-vis its sacrificial dimension. The understanding of eucharistic sacrifice upon which
Anglicans, Lutherans, and Roman Catholics have agreed is that in the eucharist,
Christ's sacrifice on the cross is made present. One can agree to this principle without
thereby claiming that the primary purpose of the eucharist is to forgive the individual
sins of those present at any given eucharist, and without denying the efficacy of the confession and absolution that preceded the communion.

6. *1 Apology* 66.

7. Book of Common Prayer, p. 858.

nant with this view.[8] The common denominator of forgiveness, regeneration, and new life is union with God through Christ. Forgiveness and reconciliation are the preconditions, and indeed the threshhold, of rebirth and regeneration, but the content of our new lives in Christ is union. We were created and destined for nothing less than this life of intimacy with God.

While the Prayer Book catechism does not specify the connection between baptism and the eucharist, their relation is readily extrapolated by putting together the statement previously rehearsed about baptism with its counterpart regarding the eucharist, whose benefits are said to be "the forgiveness of our sins, the strengthening of our union with Christ and one another, and the foretaste of the heavenly banquet which is our nourishment in eternal life."[9] There is some significant overlap here: both baptism and eucharist function to forgive sin, and both unite us to God and other members of Christ's body. Yet each of the sacraments also seems to have a particular function: new life in the Spirit appears to be the special province of baptism, as the foretaste of heaven is that of the eucharist.[10]

If we turn to the question of how confession is related to the eucharist, the pattern becomes somewhat more complex, if only because while the view of baptism and eucharist just presented would be acceptable to a large number of Christians, any view of confession is apt to be much more debatable. Nevertheless, let us point to the fact that the notion one makes a confession of sin before the eucharist is both ancient, going back as far as the *Didache* and widespread, penitential rites at the beginning of the eucharist having become the norm in the West.[11] Contemporary eucharistic rites of many traditions begin with an order of confession and absolution or declaration of par-

---

8. *Catechism of the Catholic Church* (Mahwah, NJ: Paulist, 1994), nos. 1263 and 1265, pp. 321 and 322. Luther's Small Catechism in *The Book of Concord: The Confessions of the Evangelical Lutheran Church,* tr. and ed. Theodore G. Tappert (Philadelphia: Fortress Press, 1959), 348-349; in the Large Catechism, pp. 438, 441-442.

9. Book of Common Prayer, pp. 859-860.

10. Geoffrey Wainwright treats this dimension of the eucharist extensively in *Eucharist and Eschatology, passim,* but esp. ch. 2.

11. As noted, the earliest eucharistic liturgies did not themselves contain penitential rites, however, as the Liturgy of St. John Chrysostom used by the Orthodox churches today does not, beyond a petition for peace and repentance in the litany immediately preceding the Great Entrance.

don: this is the rule rather than the exception.[12] This practice of confession before communion is consonant with, and no doubt based
upon, Paul's warning about self-examination in 1 Corinthians 11:27-
34. The warning in this passage is manifold: against receiving in an
unworthy manner, of eating and drinking without discerning the body
or without judging ourselves truly and effectively, and against confus-
ing the eucharist with the family dinner. Paul casts the net much
wider than simple confession of sins, then, but this element is certainly included. Christ's own words, recorded solely by St. Matthew,
are even stronger: "So when you are offering your gift at the altar, if
you remember that your brother or sister has something against you,
leave your gift there before the altar and go; first be reconciled to your
brother or sister and then come and offer your gift" (5:23-24). While
Christ is not here speaking specifically of the eucharist, his words are
obviously applicable. They are mirrored by the restoration to the practice of many churches of the ancient custom of exchanging the peace
either immediately before the offertory and anaphora or immediately
after the anaphora but before communion.[13] While the peace in contemporary churches often degenerates into an ante-coffee hour, its
real significance is reconciliation.[14]

If we want to say, with St. Matthew, that Christ's blood is poured
out for the forgiveness of sins, it nevertheless makes little sense to say
that forgiveness is granted when we receive communion if we have already recited a formula of confession, the celebrant has declared absolution or pardon, and we have been reconciled to our neighbor in the
peace. To say that the eucharist itself is the medium of forgiveness effectively undermines what has already taken place in the penitential
rite and the peace and moreover obscures the fact that the fellowship
of those who have been reconciled is the eucharist's precondition.[15] If

12. Book of Common Prayer, Lutheran Book of Worship, Roman Sacramentary of
Paul VI. See also Calvin's eucharistic liturgy in *Prayers of the Eucharist: Early and Reformed*, tr. and ed. R. C. D. Jasper and G. J. Cuming (New York: Pueblo, 1980), 216.

13. Regarding the kiss of peace as part of the eucharistic rite of the early church,
see Wainwright, *Doxology*, 3. For its social and communal implications, see p. 143 and
note 606, p. 529. For a modern view, see Gordon Lathrop, *Holy Things: A Liturgical Theology* (Minneapolis: Fortress Press, 1993), 130.

14. Cp. Cyril of Jerusalem, *Lectures* V.3, p. 72. Justin Martyr also mentions the kiss
of peace as part of the rite of baptism and first communion, immediately preceding the
anaphora, *1 Apology* 65.

15. Cf. Senn, *Christian Liturgy*, 98. Senn documents the presence of the confession

we have already been forgiven, the communion itself can only be understood as carrying the baptized and forgiven forward from the abatement of hostility to God and neighbor towards something else, indeed, something greater. As one eucharistic prayer entreats: "Deliver us from the presumption of coming to this Table for solace only, and not for strength; for pardon only, and not for renewal. Let the grace of this Holy Communion make us one body, one Spirit in Christ."[16] Indeed, the peace and the communion may be said to unite, not only those separated by the enmity of sin, but by the very isolation of confession, as Charles Williams writes in his poem "At the 'Ye That Do Truly'" (a reference to the priest's introduction to the confession in the eucharistic rite of the 1662 Prayer Book):

> Now are our prayers divided, now
> Must you go lonelily, and I;
> For penitence shall disallow
> Communion and propinquity
> . . . .
> Death shall our marriage vows unbind,
> Death, and this sharp foretaste of death.[17]

To illustrate the breadth of theological support for the unitive dimension of the eucharist I have been urging, I will draw on the work of two theologians, selected from different strands of the Christian tradition. The first is Thomas Aquinas. In the history of battles over this, the feast of peace, Thomas's name has been associated with the doctrine of transubstantiation, which has not proved notably helpful in bringing Christians together at the altar, although its merits as a theory of how Christ is present in the elements are considerable. The battles over what God does with the elements have obscured a peace over what God does with us, as we shall see,

---

in the early Lutheran liturgies, noting that Luther took the peace to be an absolution for the sins of those about to commune (p. 278; cf. also pp. 338, 351-352, 407, and 412). There were also confessions in early Reformed liturgies (p. 367), and of course, in the 1549 and 1662 versions of the Book of Common Prayer. F. D. Jouret sees the eucharist as remitting venial sins, but only because it increases charity within us, and only charity combined with regret for sin is a sufficient remedy for venial sin; see *The Eucharist and the Confessional* (Westminster, MD: Newman Press, [n.d.]), 126-128.

16. Book of Common Prayer, Eucharistic Prayer C, p. 372.
17. Charles Williams, *Divorce* (London: H. Milford, 1920).

for regarding the effect of the sacraments, there is greater unanimity than one might suppose.

Thomas's notion of the effect of the sacrament is elaborated in several places, in his treatment of the effects of the sacraments generally, the effects specifically of the eucharist, and in the breviary lesson he wrote for the feast of Corpus Christi. In his treatment of the sacraments in general in the larger *Summa* (III.62 and 63), Thomas's short answer to the question of the effect of the sacraments is: grace.[18] Yet this answer is merely the short form of a longer thought, the conclusion of an extended line of reasoning. The sacraments cause grace because through them humanity "is incorporated with Christ." If none but God can cause grace, it is not because Thomas is here worried about the spectre of Pelagianism, but because of what he takes grace to be, "nothing else than a participated likeness of the Divine Nature,"[19] and he then quotes 2 Peter 1:4, the standard patristic proof text of deification. Because the sacraments derive their power from the passion, their effect is also that "the virtue of [the Passion] is in a manner united to us by our receiving the sacraments,"[20] and thus, by faith Christ dwells in us and we are united to him by his power.[21]

These effects of the sacraments generally are also specifically the effects of the eucharist, as Thomas later attests. On this point, however, Thomas prefers to speak through quotation of Cyril of Jerusalem: " 'God's life-giving Word by uniting Himself with His own flesh, made it to be productive of life. For it was becoming that He should be united somehow with bodies through His sacred flesh and precious blood.' " Thomas finds a similar theme in Augustine, whom he likewise quotes: " 'O sacrament of piety, O sign of unity, O bond of charity.' "[22] Between them, these quotations from Cyril and Augustine suggest three kinds of unity: the hypostatic union of natures in Christ, Christ's bodily union with us in the reception of the consecrated elements, and the bond of charity that unites us to one another as well as to God.

In building upon this theory of union, Thomas goes so far as to

18. Aquinas, *Summa*, III, 62, 1 *s.c.* The translation here follows that of the English Dominican Province (Westminster, MD: Christian Classics, 1981 [rpt.]).
19. Aquinas, *Summa*, III, 62, 1 resp.
20. Aquinas, *Summa*, III, 62, 5 resp.
21. Aquinas, *Summa*, III, 62, 5 ad 2.
22. Aquinas, *Summa*, III, 79, 1 resp.

downplay the eucharist's connection to satisfaction for sin: "Through the power of the sacrament it produces directly that effect for which it was instituted. Now it was instituted not for satisfaction, but for nourishing spiritually through union between Christ and His members, as nourishment is united with the person nourished."[23] Indeed, in this respect, Thomas draws a sharp contrast between baptism and the eucharist: "Baptism is given to a man as dying with Christ, whereas the Eucharist is given as by way of nourishing and perfecting him through Christ."[24]

Such nourishment and perfection indeed bear a relation to forgiveness of sins, and the reason is indicated by the earthly banquet's relation to the mystical banquet of the Age to Come: "It belongs to this sacrament to cause the attaining of eternal life. Because it was by His Passion that Christ opened to us the approach to eternal life."[25] While the sacrament does not afford us such immediate union with God that the New Age could be said to have dawned, it is the means of our getting there: "This sacrament does not at once admit us to glory, but bestows on us the power of coming unto glory."[26] Since in the next life we will be free from sin (as Augustine would have it, possessing the ultimate freedom of not being able to sin), we must assume that the eucharist, the sacrament that carries us forward to this new life, presupposes purification from sin. If the sacrament unites us to Christ, to one another, and to glory, it must also bear some relation to cleansing: the unholy may not be joined to the Holy, nor can a bond of charity be said to exist in any meaningful sense between those estranged by offense. Thomas's eucharistic theology suggests, as does the liturgical pattern, that the eucharist begins where repentance and pardon leave off; on this reading, the eucharist is intrinsically related to these latter, is indeed dependent upon them, but it is not said to repeat them.

This point is made more strongly in the breviary lesson Thomas composed for the feast of the eucharist, Corpus Christi. There he stresses again the intent of the eucharist as deification, participation in divine nature, echoing what Irenaeus, Athanasius, and Gregory Nazianzen all say of the matter: Christ took our nature on himself, be-

---

23. Aquinas, *Summa*, III, 79, 5 resp.
24. Aquinas, *Summa*, III, 79, 5 ad 1.
25. Aquinas, *Summa*, III, 79, 2 resp.
26. Aquinas, *Summa*, III, 79, 2 ad 1.

coming human that he might make us divine.[27] The effects of the sacrament form a long list: the bread and wine, he says, are nourishment,
memorial, faith's opportunity, the gift of health, purgation from sin,
the mind's fortification, and, above all, the means by which Christ's
love is brought home to the hearts of the faithful, and their joy. It
seems that Thomas is reluctant to separate forgiveness of sins from
spiritual growth, yet it would be more accurate to say that his view of
the eucharist posits regeneration as its effect than that it claims forgiveness of sin alone, or even principally. Indeed, the fact that Thomas
here uses the classic language of deification indicates that the chief ru-
bric of his eucharistic theology is union with God.[28]

Conventional wisdom would hold that in turning from Aquinas to
our next theologian we would encounter stark contrast. This view is
not wholly mistaken, for Calvin's theology appears to deemphasize
the sacraments as *means* of grace. He begins from the definition of a
sacrament that ultimately reverts to Augustine (a visible sign of an invisible grace)[29] focusing on the first part concerning the outward
sign.[30] Nevertheless, he does cite the latter part of the definition, saying that a sacrament is "a visible form of an invisible grace,"[31] and
claims that his definition differs from Augustine's only in being more
understandable to the ordinary Christian.

If one were, on the basis of this definition, inclined to doubt Calvin's conviction of the unitive nature of the sacraments, his treatment
of both baptism and the eucharist must dispel this suspicion. The purpose and effect of both baptism and eucharist are humanity's union
with God: "For as in baptism, God, regenerating us, engrafts us into
the society of his church, and makes us his own by adoption, so . . .
[he continually supplies] to us the food to sustain and preserve us in
that life to which he has begotten us by his Word." The eucharist,

---

27. An English translation of the office reading may be found in *Thomas Aquinas:
Theological Texts*, tr. Thomas Gilby (Durham, NC: Labyrinth, 1982), 365-366.

28. For a fuller explication of the relation between deification and union in
Thomas's work, see A. N. Williams, *The Ground of Union: Deification in Aquinas and
Palamas* (New York: Oxford University Press, 1999).

29. Augustine, *De catechizandis rudibus* 50.

30. John Calvin, *Institutes of the Christian Religion* IV.xiv.1; the translation cited here
is that of Ford Lewis Battles (Philadelphia: Westminster, 1960).

31. Calvin, *Institutes* IV.xiv.1. Note that adoption is virtually synonymous with deification and union in patristic theology (see A. N. Williams, *Ground of Union*, 27-32) and
in medieval and Byzantine theology (chs. 2, 3, and 4).

then, sustains us in that sharing in divine life begun when in baptism we were made God's own by grace. Yet more specifically, Calvin speaks of the eucharist as a "mystery of Christ's secret union with the devout."[32] We are "so united to Christ himself that we become sharers in all his blessings." Indeed, he even seems to reverse the order one might expect, making regeneration the fruit of union.[33] The eucharist differs from baptism chiefly in being intended as a continuing nourishment, rather than a once-for-all declaration of our belonging to God; in this respect Calvin's thought lies close to Thomas's. The eucharist, however, just as much as baptism, makes us participants in divine nature: "Our heavenly Father invites us to Christ, that, refreshed by partaking of him, we may repeatedly gather strength until we shall have reached heavenly immortality."[34]

In seeing the effects of the sacraments in this way, Calvin is, as a good theologian should be, merely showing the working out of the Christology he earlier affirmed, for this doctrine of union is already there; of the blessing of Christ's kingly office, he writes: "Hence we are furnished . . . with the gifts of the Spirit, which we lack by nature. By these first fruits we may perceive that we are truly joined to God in perfect blessedness,"[35] and "Christ stands in our midst, to lead us little by little to a firm union with God."[36] The purpose of the incarnation was that humanity might be united to God and therefore this is also the purpose of the sacraments instituted by Christ.

Calvin and Thomas both point us to the multiplicity of unities suggested by the eucharist, and it is to a fuller exploration of these that I now turn. The basis for union we have seen quite clearly in both theologians: we may be united to God because of the supreme moment of such union, which is Christ himself. This christological basis for asserting humanity's union with God becomes particularly important in the context of the eucharist. If Christ had not been human, he could not have taken bread, blessed it, broken it, given thanks, and said "This is my body," in the first instance simply because he would have had no body. Yet conversely, had he not been divine, the eucharist would become at best meaningless and at worst, cannibalistic.

32. Calvin, *Institutes* IV.xvii.1.
33. Calvin, *Institutes* IV.xv.6.
34. Calvin, *Institutes* IV.xvii.1
35. Calvin, *Institutes* II.xv.4.
36. Calvin, *Institutes* II.xv.5.

The Last Supper makes sense, as do all the eucharists after it, solely because of the hypostatic union of natures, human and divine, in Christ. This is both logically the first kind of union associated with the eucharist, inasmuch as without it, there would be no eucharist at all, and also the foremost, in that the union of natures in Christ's person is the most intimate of the many to which the eucharist alludes and is the one in which all others are rooted.

Conversely, it is the eucharist that leads us to understand the hypostatic union in Christ. As the disciples on the road to Emmaus could not recognize the risen Lord until the breaking of the bread (Luke 24:13-31), so his later disciples are given the eucharist that they also may understand. As the incarnation itself can be taken as the moment of God's greatest self-disclosure and self-explication to humanity, so the eucharist, if we extend this line of reasoning, now represents the fullest moment of our apprehension of God's embodiment, for in it every Christian, and not only those of first-century Palestine, knows Christ in the flesh, and experiences the incarnation of the Word. When Thomas doubted, Jesus offered his body as proof of his identity (John 20:24-29), and to believers in the centuries of the church, he offers his body, that through it, we may know who he is. Here, too, is union, for as Augustine took knowledge to be the mind's conformity to the thing known,[37] so our knowledge of God binds our minds to God.

The eucharist brings about not only intellectual, but also physical, union, for while Christ remains the sole instance of a hypostatic union, through the eucharist the union of God and humanity is realized manifold in the bodies of the saints. The eucharist is thus both the manifestation of Christ's corporeality and manifestation of the intimacy of the union to which God invites humankind. God's methods are undeniably crude: the incarnate One blesses bread and wine, telling us that these are he himself, and then suggests that we eat him. Indeed, in the Gospel of St. John he goes so far as to say the direst consequences will result if we do *not* eat him (John 6:53). As St. Cyril of Jerusalem writes: "By partaking of the Body and Blood of Christ [you will] be made of the same body and the same blood with him. For thus we come to bear Christ in us, because His Body and Blood are diffused through our members."[38] The act of eating effects our un-

37. Augustine, *De Trinitate* IX.16.
38. Cyril of Jerusalem, *Lectures* IV.3, p. 68.

ion with God: the body united with a divine nature is now united with us, and united with us precisely in a bodily act. In the liturgy of the Book of Common Prayer, communicants are reminded of this union as they recite the Prayer of Humble Access: "Grant us therefore, gracious Lord, so to eat the flesh of thy dear Son Jesus Christ, and to drink his blood, that we may evermore dwell in him and he in us,"[39] and thus the Eucharist becomes the door to a mutual indwelling.[40]

If there is crudity in this carnal union, it must exist at the level of the first odd idea, which was to create a material world and embodied creatures in the first place. The act of eating merely follows from this: if these material beings destined for fellowship with the uncircumscribed deity are indeed to be united with God, then that union cannot represent any escape on their part from the embodied state in which God, incomprehensibly perhaps, created them. Like the resurrection, the eucharist tells us indubitably that we are meant to be embodied and that our progress in the spiritual life can only include bodily blessing as well as bodily discipline. Our union with God, now and forever, is as physical as a human marriage. Indeed, Christ's first miracle, the marriage at Cana, foretells the eucharist: as Christ himself supplies wine for a feast of union, so later in the Upper Room, in the form of wine he will give himself for union.

By foreshadowing the Last Supper, the marriage at Cana (John 2:1-11) tells us much about the eucharist. First, it shows us that God is intent on bodily union by placing Mary at the center of the narrative and thus at the beginning of Jesus' public ministry. It is appropriate that Mary urge her son to supply wine on this occasion, the harbinger of the eucharistic feasts to come, for she is the first sign of corporeal union in our midst. Mary's situation in one sense is unique: no one but she is united to God in the way that she was between the Annunciation and the Nativity. Nevertheless, her presence and role at Cana remind us that God wills to be united to all of us, and indeed, bodily united, and that this union shows forth humanity's great dignity in the sight of God. Above all, it testifies to that unitive force which is the love of God.[41] If we honor Mary it is because, as the Council of

---

39. Book of Common Prayer, Rite I, p. 337.

40. John Macquarrie, *A Guide to the Sacraments* (New York: Continuum, 1998), 49.

41. This definition derives from the Pseudo-Dionysius (*Divine Names* 4) and is later picked up by Aquinas both in his treatment of the one God (*Summa* I, 20, 1 ad 3) and in that of the Holy Spirit (I, 38, 1 obj. 3 and ad 3).

Ephesus proclaimed, she is the Theotokos (God-Bearer), and in honoring her, we seek to honor the God who condescended to be united with us in the flesh and born of human flesh, that we might become the adopted children of God. This first miracle reminds us, through Mary, of Christ's enfleshment and of Christ's blessing on our flesh, even those desires of the flesh that are fulfilled by marriage and wine. Mary reminds us that the Christian saga is precisely a divine comedy: although her soul is to be pierced (Luke 2:35), the marriage at Cana stands as testament to the fact that she knows her son is for feasting. The miracle of this wedding feast both anticipates the Last Supper and all the eucharists that recollect it, and points to the unitive good of the eucharist, which like a marriage is both bodily and spiritual, and like a wedding feast, celebrates both God's blessing and human joy.

The incarnation, then, grounds all humanity's union with God, but specifically points to personal union, a union that is ours through the eucharist. In accepting this union in and of the person, we are reminded that our whole selves, including our bodies, are made by God for himself, and our whole selves, including our bodies, minds, and souls, are granted union with God, the starkest sign of which is God's bodily union with us in the womb of a woman and under the forms of bread and wine.

The incarnation points toward and fosters another kind of unity, one that is ours with the blessed society that is the Trinity. Modern eucharistic prayers commonly make this point: addressed to the First Person, they recall the Second Person's incarnation, crucifixion, resurrection, and gift of self at the Last Supper, and call upon the Spirit to make Christ present at this particular altar now, in this gathering of latter-day saints.[42] The eucharist, then, is not only the Supper of the

---

42. Not all eucharistic prayers take this form, and some very ancient ones were addressed to the Son: cf. Senn, *Christian Liturgy*, 83. This is a point of dispute between Jungmann and Albert Gerhards (see "Prière addressée à Dieu ou au Christ?: Relecture d'une thèse importante de J. A. Jungmann à la lumière de la recherche actuelle," in *Liturgie, Spiritualité, Cultures*, ed. A. M. Triacca and A. Pistoia, Bibliotheca Ephemerides Liturgicae; subsidia 29 (Rome: Edizioni Liturgiche, 1983), 101-114. Nevertheless, this form is the most usual today in modern Western liturgies and is the form of the eucharistic prayer in the Liturgy of St. John Chrysostom. Allan Bouley regards the development of explicitly trinitarian structures in the anaphora as the positive by-product of doctrinal development towards what is today considered orthodoxy; see *From Freedom to Formula: The Evolution of the Eucharistic Prayer from Oral Improvisation to Written Texts*, Catholic University of America Studies in Christian Antiquity; no. 21 (Washington, DC:

Lamb, but the Trinity's own high feast. In the eucharist we recall the
Trinity's will that we be sanctified and celebrate the work of the undivided Three in the history of salvation. Above all, we feast with the
Trinity, in the company of the hosts of heaven, as we receive the One
who by the Father's will and the Spirit's power came and dwelt among
us as one of us.

In recalling the Three as the celebrant recounts the acts of Christ
on the night before he died, we recall their perfect distinction in unity.
As the anaphora addresses the Father, we remember that the First Person is the source and fount of the Trinity; in the recitation of Christ's
saving deeds, we are reminded that it is the Second Person who becomes incarnate; in calling upon the Spirit to descend and sanctify the
gifts, we remember that since the Ascension, God is made present in
our midst through the work of the Third. In recalling each of the
Three, though, we are also simultaneously reminded of their unity
and mutuality, for all work to the common end of accomplishing our
union with God. As one eucharistic prayer succinctly puts it: "We pray
you gracious God [the Father], to send your Holy Spirit upon these
gifts that they may be the sacrament of the Body of Christ and his
Blood of the new Covenant."[43] The unity of the trinitarian work of salvation and sanctification is further underlined in their concluding
doxologies: "All this we ask through your Son Jesus Christ. By him,
and with him, and in him, in the unity of the Holy Spirit all honor and
glory is yours, Almighty Father, now and forever. Amen."[44] The
eucharist thus invites us to contemplation of the Trinity, to its perfect
unity in distinction. If we take seriously perichoresis, the mutual
interpenetration of the Three, then we also know that even as we partake of Christ's body and blood, we also participate in the life of the
Trinity, life that is itself perfect and divine communion.

If the incarnation represents the moment of greatest transparency
in God's self-revelation, the point of God's greatest intelligibility to

---

Catholic University of America Press, 1981), 249-251. It is the structure of all the
anaphoras of the Book of Common Prayer, and well as Eucharistic Prayers I and II in the
Lutheran Book of Worship. One may dispute whether the Trinitarian structure of these
prayers is sufficiently transparent in view of the catechetical function of the liturgy: cf.
Bryan D. Spinks, "Trinitarian Theology and the Eucharistic Prayer," *Studia Liturgica* 26
(1996): 209-224.

43. Book of Common Prayer, Eucharistic Prayer B, p. 369.
44. Book of Common Prayer, Eucharistic Prayer 1, p. 363.

us, it also represents a window onto the Trinity. It is a mistakenly christocentric piety that regards the Gospels and the eucharist as a means of relation with Christ as an end in itself, a piety that misunderstands Christ in isolating him from the Father and the Spirit. We receive of the eucharist not solely that we may know the Second Person who became flesh, but so that through his body, we may understand the God whom we adore, the Three in One and One in Three.

In contemplating the communion of Persons in the Trinity, we are reminded of a third kind of unity forged and expressed in the communion in bread and wine: the unity of the human persons who together partake of bread and wine. The eucharist is in its truest form a synaxis, a gathering together of a community. Here is the point at which the inseparability of the eucharist from confession becomes crucial. The community that partakes of the eucharist is the community of the baptized, those who have been washed of the stain of original sin, yet they are also those who sin, and who therefore must confess and experience pardon before they may make any offering to God. Here is the paradox: the community that gathers is at once regenerate and sinful. It gathers because it consists of those who at baptism have received the gospel, been marked with the sign of the cross and declared Christ's own forever, yet in hearing the gospel, each member also hears Christ's word to leave our gift at the altar and be reconciled to those from whom we are estranged (Matt. 5:23-24). In reciting a formula of confession, we recall our sin against both God and neighbor, as well as our need for repentance. We are reminded also of the imperative to renewal of life and conversion of manners: we are not given pardon so that we may continue to live unholy lives, but so that we may take heart, turn, and sin no more. It is confession that enables us to exchange the peace, and the exchange of peace which makes us into the kind of community that can break the sacred bread together, but the confession and peace have no meaning if we stop with them: "peace on earth, goodwill to all" was surely meant to mean more than the mere absence of hostility, as confession is meant to do more than dispatch past fault. In the Christian vision, repentance grants new life; it carries the penitent forward, rather than simply leaving her able to live with her past, its sins and errors.[45]

---

45. Cp. Macquarrie, *Guide to the Sacraments*, 96: "The sacrament of penance, as a means of grace, is not just to assure us of the forgiveness of specific sins but to bring us into a closer relation to God."

The fullness of forgiveness is renewal, and Christian repentance is thus concerned with the future quite as much as, and perhaps more than, with the past.

If reconciliation is the minimal condition of the assembly's unity, it is the eucharist that turns this collection of merely unhostile people into something that can genuinely be called a community.[46] Thus Paul reasons from the sharing in the bread and cup to the constitution of the community: "The cup of blessing which we bless, is it not a sharing in the blood of Christ? The bread which we break, is it not a sharing in the body of Christ? Because there is one bread, we who are many are one body, for we all partake of the one bread" (1 Cor. 10:16-17), words which have entered into at least one modern eucharistic liturgy.[47] There is ancient precedent both for this notion itself and its explicit statement within the eucharistic rite, as in the anaphora of the Byzantine Liturgy of Saint Basil, when the priest prays: "Unite with one another all of us who partake of the one bread and the cup into fellowship with the one Holy Spirit."[48] The human act is that repentance which opens the way for union, the divine act the actual creation of unity in the community, effected by the communion and based upon the hypostatic union in Christ.

The community that gathers at the table remembering the gracious self-giving of the Triune God is thus brought with the greatest intimacy into that triune life. The perfect community on whom the anaphora calls is at once the sign under which the community gathers and the sign of that to which it is called: the church is meant to mirror the perfection of community that is the Trinity, and the eucharist is meant to create that perfection. Despite the radical difference between God and humanity, between the divine Persons' participation in one nature and the human community's union through grace, we may nevertheless legitimately claim an analogy between the communion of the Trinity and that of the church. The unity of nature that the Christian tradition has wanted to assert of the Three Persons is balanced by an equal insistence that they are distinct from one another; indeed distinction is one of the minimal conditions of being a person, in the

46. Cp. Schmemann's assertion that the eucharist is the sacrament of the assembly, and hence the sacrament of the church; *The Eucharist: Sacrament of the Kingdom,* tr. Paul Kachur (Crestwood, NY: St. Vladimir's, 1988), 13.

47. The otherwise execrable New Zealand Prayer Book.

48. *Prayers of the Eucharist,* 120.

definition of *person* most common in the West. (A person, according to Boethius, is an individual substance of a rational nature.)[49] The fact that the tradition has found it difficult to articulate the precise nature of that distinctiveness should not obscure the fact that it has wanted to affirm distinction. Indeed, without distinction, we cannot posit unity, but only identity. So the church is a union of those who are really distinct, and far from obliterating distinction, the union presupposes it. That is precisely the divinely-wrought mystery.

In differing but analogous ways, then, both the Trinity and the church are meant to be communities of persons, societies where distinction and unity are held in balance so that one does not obliterate the other. As communities they are said to exist in virtue of their unity; as communities of specifically persons, they exist in virtue of their constituents' being really distinct. In calling on and recalling the work of the Three in the anaphora, the celebrant speaks to and for the community, reminding it of its corporate nature. If we are made in the image of God, as the anaphora reminds us, then we are made for such unity-in-distinction.

Not only the liturgy at the altar, but also the liturgy of the Word proclaims this communal dimension, for as we recite the Nicene Creed we are reminded, lest we forget, that the community of which we are part is defined by a commonly-held belief, not by the parameters of the present gathering, and so extends through space and time. Indeed, the liturgy specifically bids us recall this unity by alluding to the communion of saints near the beginning of the anaphora: "Therefore we praise you, joining our voices with Angels and Archangels and with all the company of heaven, who for ever sing this hymn to proclaim the glory of your Name."[50] Every eucharist, then, is the great high feast of the glorious company of heaven, and in this proclamation the eucharist affirms that death has been destroyed. The corollary of the destruction of death is the reality of the community's unity through time. While those who stand around the altar will (in all likelihood) taste death before the coming of the kingdom, in this moment and act of praise, they are united to the heavenly host, the cherubim and seraphim, the glorious company of apostles, the noble fellowship of prophets, the white-robed army of martyrs, and the holy church

49. Boethius, *De duabus naturis* 3.
50. Book of Common Prayer, Eucharistic Prayers A and B, pp. 362 and 367.

throughout the world, in the words of the Te Deum, which may originally have been a eucharistic prayer.[51] The eucharist proclaims that the rupture in time which is death has been healed, that the severance of the faithful through death has been overcome. Hence St. Ignatius can refer to the eucharist as the medicine of immortality.[52] Most of all, the eucharist both proclaims and makes real this central fact of Christian existence: that the baptized who now commune have already died and risen again. The death that is yet to come does not define us, but is rather our last trial along the road to the heavenly banquet. So in each celebration of the eucharist, we not only know the wound of death to have been healed but are also for a moment made one with the heavenly host. This, too, is reconciliation: the reunion of those severed by death and scattered throughout time.

The celebratory cry of the Sanctus, in which join the living and the departed saints, as well as the angelic host, suggests yet another kind of unity wrought by the eucharist: the unity of the cosmos. Saints and angels are quite different kinds of creatures, and while we shall, God willing, one day join the ranks of the saints, we can never become angels. The heavenly chorus to which we add our many voices at every eucharist is thus a mixed choir, one composed of vastly different kinds of creatures. This point is expressed even more clearly in a eucharistic prayer whose origins lie in the Liturgy of Saint Basil, variants of which are used by a wide variety of Christians today.[53] In the version of the Book of Common Prayer, the celebrant says: "Countless throngs of angels stand before you to serve you night and day; and, beholding the glory of your presence, they offer you unceasing praise. Joining with them, and giving voice to every creature under heaven, we acclaim you, and glorify your Name."[54] Here it is not only human beings and angels who praise God, but rational beings who use their gift of speech on behalf of all the diverse creatures whom God has made, ra-

51. See Marion J. Hatchett, *Commentary on the American Prayer Book* (San Francisco: HarperSanFrancisco, 1995), 117.

52. Ignatius, *Ephesians* 20.

53. It is known throughout the Eastern Orthodox world, as well as in one of the Oriental Orthodox churches (the Coptic) in an emended form; it is also known to Roman Catholics as one of the four eucharistic prayers of the Roman sacramentary of Paul VI, as well as in the American Book of Common Prayer, and forms of it have been authorized by the Inter-Lutheran Commission on Worship, by the United Methodist Church, and by the Consultation on Church Union.

54. Book of Common Prayer, Eucharistic Prayer D, p. 373.

tional and nonrational, made in the image of God and not so made. This is not the heavenly host singing, but the entire creaturely host on heaven and on earth, united for a moment in what may legitimately be called the hymn of the universe.

These various unities — of natures in Christ, of the persons of the Trinity, of human persons with one another, and of humanity with God — could all be said, in one way or another, to point to an underlying unity, one that has particular significance for the life of the church. This fundamental unity is that of charity and truth. In the thought of both St. Augustine and St. Thomas, these are inextricably united for two quite different reasons. The first is that in the simple nature of God, charity and truth are the same. As Thomas explains, we give different names to these because our language reflects the experience of composite creatures living in a composite world, and to the extent that discrete terms imply distinction in the simple, divine nature, our language falls short of complete accuracy.[55] The second reason, yet more significant in the context of the eucharist, is grounded in an ancient understanding of the Trinity. In the thought of St. Augustine, which was later adopted and expanded by St. Thomas, knowledge and charity are the proper qualities of the Second and Third Persons of the Trinity respectively, as origination is that of the First Person. As the Persons of the Trinity are distinct, yet perfectly united, so are charity and knowledge in God.[56]

Inasmuch as in the eucharist we partake of the divine nature, then we partake of that simple nature in which charity and truth are identical. Inasmuch as in the eucharist we partake of the divine and trinitarian life to which Christ was sent to witness, we partake of charity and truth united inseparably as Father, Son, and Spirit are united. The liturgy reminds us that the eucharistic community is meant to mirror this divine and trinitarian life: immediately before the offertory, we recite the Nicene Creed, which reminds us of the truths we profess, and reminds us also therefore that this community is in the first instance a group of

55. Aquinas, *Summa*, I, 13.

56. For an explication of Augustine's thought on this matter see A. N. Williams, "Contemplation: the Knowledge of God in Augustine's *De Trinitate*," in *Knowing God*, ed. James Buckley and David Yeago (Grand Rapids: Eerdmans, forthcoming). When Thomas takes up the idea, he tends to interpret the Second Person as intellect (the faculty of knowing), rather than as knowledge (the product of the faculty); nevertheless, the essential idea remains the same. Cf. *Summa*, I, 34, 1 and 2; I, 37, 1. On unity and distinction, see *Summa*, I, 28, 1 and 4; I, 31, 1; and I, 39, 1 and 2.

people whose commonality lies in their common affirmation of certain things as true. Following confession, we share the peace, thus reminding ourselves that we are meant to be bound to one another in charity. The fact that these parts of the rite precede the communion in modern Western rites suggests that charity and truth are the precondition of the eucharistic meal. The anaphora itself also makes this point to one degree or another in most of its modern Western versions. In being addressed to the Father, recalling the passion, death, and resurrection of the Son, and calling upon the Spirit to bless and sanctify the gifts, it reminds the participants, first, that both the eucharist and the Christian life in general have their origin and their continuing sanctification in the Three united and not in any one of the Persons; second, that faith is directed toward the divine Persons as its object; and third, that sanctification flows from the Three as their proper fruit.

The effects of the eucharist have also been conceived in terms reducible to charity and truth. In the liturgy of St. Mark, for example, after the second epiclesis, the deacon prays that the consecrated elements foster in those who partake of them faith, renewal of soul, and fellowship in eternal life (among other things).[57] Likewise, in the Liturgy of St. James at the equivalent point, the bishop prays that the gifts may bestow sanctification, bring forth good works, and strengthen the church founded on the rock of faith.[58] Eucharistic Prayers I and II in the Book of Common Prayer contain similar petitions.[59]

This unity of charity and truth, suggested by the invocation of the Trinity at the beginning of the liturgy as well as in the anaphora, the nature of the gathered community, and sometimes in the content of the rite itself, provides a poignant reminder of what the broader Christian community ought to be, the community, that is, now divided precisely as a eucharistic community. As Christ's body is broken at the fraction, so in the eucharist, Christ's body, the church, manifests its brokenness and manifests its divisions with greater clarity and poignancy than at any other time. Christians justify or live with

---

57. *Prayers of the Eucharist*, 66.

58. *Prayers of the Eucharist*, 93.

59. See Prayer A: "Sanctify us . . . that we may faithfully receive this holy Sacrament, and serve you in unity, constancy, and peace" (p. 363) and Prayer B: "In him, you have brought us out of error into truth, and out of sin into righteousness, out of death into life" (p. 368); Prayers I and II refer to our being filled with grace and "heavenly benediction" (pp. 336 and 342).

these divisions in a variety of ways. Some assert that the only valid basis for a eucharistic community is agreement about the truth. Thus, until there is doctrinal unity there can be no eucharistic sharing. This school of thought indeed seeks unity, but seeks it first, and effectively only, at the doctrinal level.[60] Another school of thought regards Christian division as scandalous, but finds the scandal can adequately be overcome by common action and appeal to charity. For this school, not only can there be eucharistic sharing without doctrinal unity, it is a sin against charity for the eucharist to be, as this school would say, "exclusive."[61] For one school, truth is the all-important content of fellowship; for the other it is charity. Both schools have grounding in the received wisdom of the Christian tradition, yet they reach conclusions that are diametrically opposed. Which is right?

The merit of the first school of thought, the one that holds doctrinal agreement to be the necessary prerequisite for eucharistic sharing, is that it takes seriously the patristic understanding of the Christian community. Early Christians were not distinguished from other communities in the ancient world by race, or class, or ethnicity; what joined these disparate people together was belief, particularly belief in the risen Lord made known in the Scriptures, the prayers, and the breaking of bread. The conjunction of belief and eucharistic sharing was emphasized by the catechumenate: not only did the uninitiated not share in the sacred meal, their dismissal at the end of the liturgy of the word meant they did not even witness the eucharist itself.[62] For this reason, participation in the eucharist has generally been taken as the completion and seal of Christian initiation.[63]

---

60. Those who would ground this position might point to the ancient assumption that confession of faith and baptism are the prerequisites for admission to the eucharist; see Justin Martyr, *1 Apology* 65 and the *Didache*.

61. For an example of advocacy of this position, see Lathrop, *Holy Things*, 131-132. Lathrop is here arguing not specifically for intercommunion, but the admission of the non-baptized to communion, but the argument he makes for the latter clearly pleads the former.

62. In the eucharistic prayer composed by Calvin, the minister not only exhorts the faithful to examine themselves before communing, but also announces that the Last Supper was a meal for the disciples and "strangers, and those who are not of the company of the faithful, ought not to be admitted"; see *Prayers of the Eucharist*, 216.

63. See Aidan Kavanagh, *The Shape of Baptism: The Rite of Christian Initiation*, Studies in the Reformed Rites of the Catholic Church vol. 1 (Collegeville, MN: Liturgical Press, 1991), 162, 176-177.

Indeed, membership in this eucharistic community was viewed as consisting not only in the privilege of being able to share in the meal, but also in the responsibility to share in sacrifice for Christ by dying for the faith. Thus Ignatius of Antioch could write, on his way to the amphitheatre in Rome, that he was God's wheat and desired the lions' teeth to grind him, that he might become the "pure bread of Christ" (*Rom.* iv). In Ignatius's view, then, participation in the eucharistic sacrifice meant both communing in the feast at the altar and, if need be, dying for Christ in the arena. Although it would be ludicrous to suggest that most Christians thought this way — martyrs were precisely the exception rather than the rule — the fact that a bishop of the church thought this way, and that the community preserved and handed on the letter in which he recorded the thought, makes clear that this connection between confessing the faith and participation in the eucharist seemed fitting.

The notion of the eucharist as the expression and bond of charity has also something to commend it, however. The liturgical evidence to which one might point here is that after the confession and peace, we proceed to the altar together. If reconciliation is the precondition of the eucharist, the actual breaking of bread together is reconciliation's seal. There can be no merely theoretical making of peace, for we are asked to eat at table together. While it is not clear that the eucharist creates a bond not already established through common faith, it is equally clear that that very common faith bids us abide in charity. Abiding in charity must mean, at the very least, that we do not rest content with our separate eucharists. If we are to say that truth requires we wait for agreement before sharing in the feast of love, charity requires at least that we be tireless in seeking the truth together, and be willing to acknowledge truth when we see it in others.

What would this principle require in practical terms? I see several possibilities. First, we need to consider seriously the effect of our ecclesial divisions on the eucharist. Here I pick up the suggestion of John Zizioulas, drawing conclusions from them that he does not state explicitly. Zizioulas views the eucharist as an act and synaxis of the local church, a catholic act of a catholic church, whose catholicity here and now is revealed in the eucharist.[64] Later, he raises the question of

---

64. John D. Zizioulas, *Being as Communion: Studies in Personhood and the Church*, Contemporary Greek Theologians no. 4 (Crestwood, NY: St. Vladimir's, 1985), 145.

whether a confessional body per se has the right to be regarded as church (note that his examples of confessional churches are Orthodox, Anglican, and Lutheran). He responds that if ecclesiality is inseparably linked with locality, then the answer is "definitely negative." To the next question, whether a local church can truly be local and a church if it is in a state of confessional division, he replies that the question is an extremely difficult one, but given the notion of local church he has developed "we must be prepared to question the ecclesial status of *confessional* churches as such, and begin to work on the basis of the nature of the local Church."[65] Nowhere, as far as I can tell, does Zizioulas explicitly claim that the eucharist is only valid when celebrated by the one church. If, however, this is true (and it is reasonable to suppose he thinks so), then on the basis of his other cautious conclusions, we would have to assume that the legitimacy of *all* eucharists is questionable in the present situation of the church.

The suggestion bears reflection: what if our divisions were the cause of such unholiness that all our offerings were worthless in God's sight? If most of us dismiss this idea out of hand, it is in this first instance because we either dismiss the divisions as unimportant or blame others for them: if only the others would see the light, and think and speak as we do, all would be well. Our eucharists must therefore be valid and the validity of theirs is not our problem. Alternatively, we deal with the divisions by denying others the status of church altogether, although there is increasingly little support for this approach in any church.

But what if it were the case that the divisions make sacrifice unacceptable to God? The Old Testament is full of warnings of God's weariness with the rites of the unholy: "Trample my courts no more; bringing offerings is futile; incense is an abomination to me. . . . Your new moons and your appointed festivals my soul hates; they have become a burden to me, I am weary of bearing them. When you stretch out your hands, I will hide my eyes from you; even though you make many prayers, I will not listen; your hands are full of blood. Wash yourselves, make yourselves clean; remove the evil of your doings from before my eyes" (Isa. 1:12-16). This sentiment is echoed elsewhere in the Old Testament, notably in 1 Samuel (15:22), Jeremiah (6:20), Hosea (6:6; 9:4), Amos (5:21-24), and in the Psalms (40:6 and 51:16-17), as well as in the New

---

65. Zizioulas, *Being as Communion,* 259-260.

Testament, in its most extended meditation on sacrifice and priesthood, the Letter to the Hebrews (Heb. 10:5-6, quoting Psalm 40). If we assume that Christian faith and practice are to be informed by the Bible, and take for granted that the Christian life is one that necessarily includes not only self-examination but also turning and sinning no more, then we must at least consider the possibility that our sin of consenting to division renders all our eucharists unholy. If deeming that no eucharist is valid in our present divided state seems to have unbearable consequences, then for that very reason we must be at least a little suspicious of our reluctance to reach this conclusion.

If we have any reason to continue to celebrate the holy mysteries, it can only be because eucharistic assemblies were ever gatherings of the sinful and that we trust that "if we confess our sins, he who is faithful and just will forgive our sins and cleanse us from all unrighteousness" (1 John 1:9). If Scripture gives us warrant for believing we can turn to God seeking the fruits of redemption, however, we cannot do so by blithely ignoring sin: "If we say we have no sin, we deceive ourselves, and the truth is not in us" (1 John 1:8). A psalm commonly recited by Christians on penitential occasions, Psalm 51, says: "Had you desired it, I would have offered sacrifice, but you take no delight in burnt offerings. The sacrifice of God is a troubled spirit; a broken and contrite heart, O God, you will not despise" (vv. 17-18, Book of Common Prayer Psalter). Perhaps the sacrifice of God required in our situation is a spirit troubled by the divisions of the church, a contrite heart broken by the brokenness of Christ's body, the church.

What are the marks of a broken and contrite heart? Liberation theology has urged us to acknowledge that sin is not only individual but also corporate. Liberation theologians have primarily applied this insight in the realm of social injustice, which is meet and right. Social injustice, however, does not exhaust the list of corporate sins, nor are corporate sins only those committed by groups. The question is not only how Christian bodies have sinned against one another in the past, although as Rowan Williams has rightly pointed out, it is high time we remember and commemorate not only the martyrs of our own confession, but also remember with contrition the martyrs our own churches made.[66] The question is also how each of us individu-

---

66. Rowan Williams, *Resurrection: Interpreting the Easter Gospel* (London: Darton, Longman & Todd, 1982), 56-58.

ally has sinned against other groups of Christians, in thought, word, and deed.

We might apply the rules of individual confession to the corporate level. Whether one makes a confession in a church that officially endorses the practice of auricular confession, or whether one simply consults a member of the clergy about a burdened conscience — a practice that is possible in any church — the operative rule, whether made explicit or not, is that one does not confess other people's sins, but one's own. One way or another, Christians take for granted the practice commended by Christ in the Gospels: that our first concern be with the logs in our own eyes, rather than the specks in other people's (Matt. 7:1-5). Like much of Jesus' advice, this is more widely commended than practiced. It remains, however, an ideal for which we surely ought to strive.

If we ought to strive for it at the individual level, why not at the corporate level also? What would such a token of repentance for disunity be, if not declining to accuse others of their failings, but instead, seeking and declaring the faults we may legitimately declare, those of our own body? In so serving the cause of charity, we would also be serving the cause of truth, for we all have something to repent. If we take seriously the principle suggested earlier, that the eucharist's role in forgiving sin is making holy, and that we cannot be forgiven unless we also consent to be made holy, then it is clear that we cannot simply celebrate the eucharist asking God's forgiveness for the body of Christ we have broken, but must also actively seek to become instruments of its healing, and the truth is restorative. We would do much to bind the wounds of Christ's body simply by speaking the truth about the failings, past and present, of our own churches.

If the eucharist is above all a sacrament of unity, then the sins it forgives must especially be corporate ones, those sins that are destructive of the body.[67] The eucharist, instituted as a sacrament of unity, now functions as the drama of division: it is precisely at this point that we see and feel most keenly the divisions in the church and the point at which many Christians most acutely experience the pain of division. This function of the eucharist as a drama of division is not

---

67. Wainwright points to growing theological stress, rooted in biblical understandings, on the eucharist as constitutive of the church and its unity; *Eucharist and Eschatology*, 115-117, 123.

entirely negative, for it is the pain occasioned by separation that provides the sharpest reminder of the existence of real divisions among Christians, of what ought not to be. To refuse the pain of separation without seeking ecclesial unity is simply to run from the consequences of sin, without actually repenting of sin. Ecclesiastical disobedience, then, when it takes the form of ignoring official guidelines regarding eucharistic participation, of seeking unity at the level of practice where it does not exist at the ecclesial and theological level, cannot help the cause of unity, and indeed, hurts it, inasmuch as it proclaims these divisions to be a matter of indifference. Of the many problems with this approach to division, I will here highlight only two. First, such practice seems to say that theology and polity are *not* constitutive of Christianity, that Christian communities exist independently of the theology they proclaim, and the structures and discipline that are both *norma normans* and *norma normata* of that theology. In so doing, they effectively sever the late twentieth century from most of the Christian past. In claiming that we best come to unity through action rather than talk, this school of thought denies the significance of thought for the Christian community and thus denies also the community's very principle of unity. Second, in refusing to accept the consequence of sin, it effectively denies that sin *is* sin and such disregard for the official rules constitutes a form of refusal to take responsibility for either the existence of the theological and ecclesial divisions themselves, or their remedy.[68]

The advocates of ecclesiastical disobedience nevertheless do remind us that we cannot simply be satisfied with matters as they are. The drama of division serves no purpose if it simply leaves us painfully aware of our wounds, with no hope of healing them. The advocates of disobedience thus pose an important question to the advocates of patience: how long? If we take the position that unity of mind must precede unity at the altar, we are still left with the question of how much unity of mind is necessary. No Christian body, not the most conservative, takes the view that variation is possible on no matters whatsoever, so it is entirely reasonable to accept the existence of some difference of theological opinion and not regard this as per se an im-

---

68. Here I differ from Wainwright, who advocates strongly for intercommunion, although without reference to the question of ecclesiastical disobedience; see *Eucharist and Eschatology,* 137-143. He may be arguing, in veiled fashion, for disobedience (146).

pediment to unity. If we acknowledge the difference between dogma and theologoumena, then we must also acknowledge that not every theological difference constitutes an impediment to eucharistic sharing. The simple appeal to the need for doctrinal agreement as the basis of eucharistic fellowship does not answer the question of precisely which issues we must settle. If we do not recognize the good of unity, and in particular, the eucharist's role as the sacrament of unity, then we might reasonably argue that we need complete unity on all issues, knowing full well that this stance will postpone table fellowship indefinitely. If, on the other hand, we do acknowledge unity as a good (albeit not a good to be bought at any price whatsoever), then we need to specify exactly *where* there needs to be doctrinal agreement, acknowledging that this should be closer to the minimum necessary than the maximum. The eucharist could then be taken both as the seal of existent doctrinal unity and as the means of grace by which God works in our midst to create greater unity among us.[69]

If in the present ecclesial climate, the adoption of such a premise seems unlikely, there is still work for the lovers of communion to do. The first task is to acknowledge the eucharist's imperative: to seek charity and truth.[70] Seeking the truth in charity means both regarding the patient work of theological dialogue as the means to unity and regarding unity as a good in itself. Seeking charity means desiring the well-being of those from whom we are separated, in virtue of the fact that we hope not to remain separated from them forever. Many churches include in their petitions at the eucharist prayers for the unity of the church; far fewer include prayers for other churches. Yet it is a travesty, surely, when at the high feast of unity, we cannot even bring ourselves to pray for those from whom we are estranged. Seeking the truth in charity means also that we eschew, both collectively and individually, cheap shots, slander, malice, *Schadenfreude*, arrogance, self-righteousness, and pride. It means regarding Paul's advice about Christian conduct as applicable to corporate speech and action, since the eucharist takes from us the possibility of acting without regard to the body: "As God's chosen ones, holy and beloved, clothe yourselves with compassion, kindness, humility, meekness,

---

69. Wainwright also speaks of the eucharist as both the expression and seal of unity; see *Doxology*, 317-319.

70. Here Wainwright's views and mine concur; see *Eucharist and Eschatology*, 143-144.

and patience. Bear with one another and, if anyone has a complaint against another, forgive each other. . . . Above all, clothe yourselves with love, which binds everything together in perfect harmony" (Col. 3:12-14). If these words apply at both the corporate and the individual level, then they apply not merely to those appointed as official good-will ambassadors and diplomats of the churches, but to what each one of us says, individually, of other groups of Christians.

Increasingly, division in the church is lived out not only at the inter-ecclesial level, but also intra-ecclesially. The huge strides forward in ecumenical agreement in the twentieth century have, sadly, paralleled increasing discord and dissent within the churches, much of it acrimonious. Those concerned at the easy dismissal of biblical and doctrinal norms need to beware lest their denunciation of laxity lead them into the trap of lovelessness and self-righteousness and thereby, to devaluation of the eucharist. That trap is an equally real danger for those who assume that any appeal to Bible or tradition is merely the fruit of intransigence or prejudice. The examination of conscience that precedes the eucharist, therefore, must also include self-scrutiny with respect to our falling short of charity in our speech and thought about those from whom we are theologically estranged, whether within our own church or outside it.

Does advocating this position mean obscuring truth for charity's sake? Absolutely not, for those who take seriously the Augustinian and Thomistic doctrine of the Trinity. The Christian way can only be one that is simultaneously true and charitable, and our inclination to see these as necessarily opposed, so that as one approaches either, one grows necessarily more distant from the other, is the result of either finitude or sin. If the eucharist is given that sin might meet its final defeat in reconciliation and love, and if it is given to bring us into that infinite generosity and graciousness that is divine life, then it must impel us to think, speak, and write in ways that manifest, or at the very least, struggle to manifest, this unity of charity and truth. No crisis in the churches can justify sin on the part of those who lament these crises. Neither the perception that the church is falling away from doctrinal or moral norms identified with truth, nor that the church is falling short of truth in its refusal to change can serve as warrant for a faithful Christian to fall away from charity in witnessing to the truth. Truth without charity is as far from the divine life of the Trinity as charity without truth.

Remembering that the eucharist is the sacrament of reconciliation and unity that has now become the drama of division means especially that we remember that Christ's body broken is not only the one on Calvary, or the one on the altar as we sing the fraction anthem, but is also the body here on earth, and the eucharist is the appropriate moment to remember that the church is not one, that the unity of which the creeds speak has not been actual for centuries and no clever or hopeful interpretation of *one* can avoid this unpleasant fact. The fraction, then, is an appropriate moment to pray to be made an instrument of God's peace in the church, and to recall that this is the appropriate prayer not for some, not for the especially designated few, but for each one of us.

The eucharist draws us toward a new vision of unity in this world by showing the passion's reproach to the sin of particularity, of regarding ourselves as safely distanced from the others. It is the seventeenth-century English mystic Thomas Traherne who has probably best expressed the universality of understanding and union toward which the eucharist draws us:

> I admire to see Thy cross in every understanding, Thy passion in every memory. Thy crown of thorns in every eye, and Thy bleeding, naked wounded [sic] body in every soul. Thy death liveth in every memory, Thy crucified person is embalmed in every affection, Thy pierced feet are bathed in every one's tears, Thy blood droppeth on every soul: Thou wholly communicatest Thyself to every soul in all kingdoms, and art wholly seen in every saint, and wholly fed upon by every Christian. It is my privilege that I can enter with Thee into every soul, and in every living temple of Thy manhood and Thy Godhead, behold again and enjoy Thy glory.[71]

To partake of Christ's flesh and blood, to look upon his wounded body, is to acknowledge the tie that binds us to all those who do likewise.

---

71. Thomas Traherne, *Centuries of Meditations* (Oxford: Clarendon, 1960), I.86. What Traherne is here locating specifically in the vision of one who feeds on Christ, other writers have seen as the effect of prayer more generally. See, for example, André Louf, *Teach Us to Pray: Learning a Little about God*, tr. Hubert Hoskins (New York: Paulist, 1975), 104-107; Pierre Teilhard de Chardin, *Le Milieu Divin: An Essay on the Interior Life* (London: Collins, 1960), 112-149; and Philip H. Pfatteicher, *Praying with the Church* (Minneapolis: Augsburg Fortress, 1995), 193-194. One of the earliest expressions of the idea is by Evagrius Ponticus, who in several ways alludes to the idea that the one who prays is connected to all other human beings, *On Prayer*, 123-126.

If the need for corporate Christian repentance is urgent in virtue of our divisions, then the eucharist stands not only as the sign that convicts conscience but also as the sign of hope, the sign of the unity of heaven where we will most perfectly enjoy the glory of God. Between the perfect community of the Age to Come and its inauguration in baptism stands the eucharist. It is at once the occasion to recall what we have to repent and to be reconciled to God and neighbor, simultaneously the most poignant moment of our divisions and the moment at which we are given a glimpse of the unity to come. Eucharists have always, we must suppose, been celebrated despite imperfect reconciliation. Yet the vision of divine and cosmic unity evoked by the eucharistic liturgy reminds us of what the eucharistic community is meant to be, will be, and in some sense, is now. If the eucharist, like baptism, imparts new life, then surely that regeneration is corporate as well as individual. If the eucharist is, in the words of the Egyptian anaphora of St. Basil, the "great mystery of godliness,"[72] then it both makes us worthy of God by sealing the forgiveness of all our sin and makes us holy by working union. The "unbloody sacrifice" does not leave us merely unhostile to God and neighbor, but promises to unite us into an image of the perfect community, the Trinity. It is to that perfection of communion that the eucharist calls.

---

72. *Prayers of the Eucharist* 71.

"I Renounce the Devil and All His Ways"

GILBERT MEILAENDER

In the translation of Luther's Small Catechism that I learned as a boy the second question in the explication of baptism reads: "What does baptism give or profit?" And the answer is: "It works forgiveness of sins, delivers from death and the devil, and gives eternal salvation to all who believe this, as the words and promises of God declare." The active agent there is baptism — or, more properly I suppose, the God who works through baptism. The person baptized is less an active agent than a recipient. There is good reason for such an emphasis, essentially the same good reason that exists for baptizing infants. Justifying faith constitutes, in fact, a moment of perfect passivity before God, who does what I am unable to do. Especially in moments of weakness and failure, I can take new heart from the fact of my baptism only if its power does not rest in any decision or choice of mine. And even in moments of strength and accomplishment, I would be a fool if I supposed that I could really create myself anew.

All along, however, the person who is and must be passive before God has been active — actively seeking and desiring, loving and longing, but these loves are inevitably disordered and idolatrous. The new identity conferred in baptism is deliverance from such disorder and freedom to love God with a whole heart. That freedom I am to reclaim daily, as the Small Catechism also makes clear. This regular reclaiming of a new identity — as one "alive to God in Christ Jesus" (Rom. 6:11) — necessarily involves an active renunciation of other possible identities and other possible lords. Nor are these other possible lords merely hypothetical. They seek to claim and possess me. They confront me with what I must acknowledge as personal will — as devil. *He,* therefore, and, alas, all his ways, must be renounced in order to fix our hearts on God, our true joy and our deepest desire. The task, therefore, is to think about the shape of this new identity conferred in baptism, the kind of renunciation to which it calls us.

My problem, however — or, at least, one of my problems — as I contemplated this topic is that the devil has too many ways among us. Moreover, these ways are highly individualized and personalized — tailored to each person's special circumstances. What constitutes stern temptation for me may have little appeal for you. Aristotle's mean is always relative to a person's character. We need, therefore, some kind of general lens through which to focus our reflection upon the devil's ways among us.

Whether I have found the best or most useful way I cannot say, but I will accomplish this focusing of our attention in a time-honored fashion. I have a text: 1 John 2:15-16. "Do not love the world or the things in the world. If any one loves the world, love for the Father is not in him. For all that is in the world, the lust of the flesh and the lust of the eyes and the pride of life, is not of the Father but is of the world." Because John's Gospel makes clear (12:31; 14:30; 16:11) that the devil is the ruler of this world, I will draw from this text a threefold schema for depicting certain ways of Satan that may tempt us and which we need to renounce: lust of the flesh, lust of the eyes, and the pride of life. I will, however, not venture down this path entirely on my own; for it is just this threefold division of temptations that St. Augustine uses in Book X (30-41) of his *Confessions,* where he takes stock of how well he is doing in the new way of life he has undertaken after that dramatic experience in the garden, when, as he puts it, "my heart was filled with a light of confidence and all the shadows of my doubt were swept away."[1] Augustine gives, therefore, a particular reading of the threefold form of temptation mentioned in 1 John, and I will use his reading as a starting point for my reflections upon the renunciations to which we today might be called.

---

1. *The Confessions of St. Augustine,* tr. Rex Warner (New York: New American Library, 1963), VIII, 12. Future references to the *Confessions* will be to this translation and will be given by book and chapter number in parentheses within the body of the text.

The Lust of the Flesh

It could be that I ought to reverse the Johannine and Augustinian order and save this category for last — thereby ensuring that you stay
with me to the very end. But that temptation I shall myself resist.
And, in fact, for Augustine, as he reflects upon the course his post-
conversion life has taken, "lust of the flesh" is a considerably broader
category than we might at first imagine. Under this heading he considers the degree to which he continues to experience temptations
originating in any of the five senses — the touch of a woman's body;
the taste of food and drink; the smell of . . . well, Augustine can name
no particular olfactory enticements that trouble him; the sound of
music whose pleasure can so overcome him as almost to obliterate
within him any attention to the words of the Psalter; the sight of beau-
tiful objects given us in both nature and culture, which objects might
easily displace God from the center of life.

In the midst of all the experiences of the senses Augustine is uncertain how to manage simultaneously love of the created good with
love of God. And we may as well grant that he probably does not always manage these intricate simultaneities perfectly. Certainly his
way of dealing with any particular temptation offered by the senses
need not be the pattern for all of us to follow. Nevertheless, the seriousness with which he takes the possibility that his soul might be
drawn away from wholehearted devotion to God, the earnestness with
which he ponders what it might mean to love God above all else, his
ever-present recognition that renunciation might be called for because
eternal issues are at stake every step along the way . . . all that de-
serves our respect and emulation.

I will not try to follow the whole of Augustine's discussion of the
temptations presented by the different senses. Instead, I will concen-
trate upon what we more commonly think of when someone mentions
"lust of the flesh," what Augustine, in Rex Warner's translation, calls
"the birdlime of concupiscence" (X, 30). When theologians propose to
say something about sex, they usually preface their remarks by noting
that it is only one area of life, that there's nothing especially bad about
it, indeed, that sexuality is God's good creation. All true, I suppose. But
it is also a powerful force for anarchy in human life. Certainly it is that
in our culture today. We need not apologize at all for thinking seriously
about what our attitude toward sexuality ought to be.

At the beginning of Book VIII of the *Confessions,* Augustine describes himself as "still closely bound by my need of woman" (VIII, 1). By the end of Book VIII, after his tumultous conversion experience and the vision of Lady Continence, Augustine can write that "you converted me to you in such a way that I no longer sought a wife . . ." (VIII, 12). For him, evidently, there was no way to manage simultaneously love of a wife and love of God. Clearly, Augustine's experience — and the renunciation he thought required — is not paradigmatic for the rest of us, but, nevertheless, there is something to be learned by reflecting upon his account.

To get at this issue we can consider what Augustine says about the pleasures of taste. Although he has, he says, "no inclination to drunkenness," he has to admit that "overeating has sometimes crept up on your servant" (X, 31). Worrying about his continued love for food, he articulates what we might call a theory of "food as medicine."

> This you have taught me, that I should have the same attitude toward taking food as I have toward taking medicine. But while I pass from the discomfort of hunger to the satisfaction of sufficiency, in that very moment of transition there is set for me a snare of concupiscence. For the moment of transition is pleasurable, and we are forced to go through that moment; there is no other way. And while we eat and drink for the sake of health, there is a dangerous kind of pleasure which follows in attendance on health and very often tries to put itself first. . . . Nor is there the same measure for both; what is enough for health is not enough for pleasure, and it is often hard to tell whether it is the necessary care of my body asking for sustenance or whether it is a deceitful voluptuousness of greed trying to seduce me. And because of this uncertainty the unhappy soul is delighted; it uses it as a cover and excuse for itself, and is glad that it is not clearly evident what is sufficient for a healthy moderation, so that under the cloak of health it may hide the business of pleasure. Every day I resist these temptations; I call upon your right hand to help me, and I refer my perplexities to you, since I have not yet found a settled plan in this matter. (X, 31)

How shall we describe Augustine's position here? We could, I think, put it this way: In the purposeful ordering of God's creation, the "good" of food is that it serves health. It sustains and nourishes life. Such nourishment is for us a necessity. We cannot avoid it; indeed, we must seek it.

It happens, however, that, as Augustine puts it, "this necessity is sweet to me" (X, 31). We enjoy eating and may sometimes take very great pleasure in it. We are tempted therefore — or so Augustine would put it — to separate the *pleasure* of eating from the *good* of eating. We may seek the pleasure for its own sake, wholly apart from the good. When that happens, Augustine seems to think, we are wrapping ourselves in the chains of necessity, and we are likely to get an ever-diminishing pleasure from an ever-increasing devotion to eating. This can happen through sheer overeating, or, more subtly perhaps, through the refined palate and exquisite sensibilities of the gourmet.

We may, I suspect, be uncertain how to react to Augustine's theory of food as medicine. There's something to it. It's worthy of reflection. But it sounds awfully moralistic, and we have the nagging suspicion that it must be all right — within some limits — just to enjoy the pleasure of eating, even when it is not connected to the need of our body for nourishment. I want to set aside these uncertainties for the moment, in order to note how Augustine treats the sexual impulse in exactly the same way as he does the impulse to eat. Rather than beginning with what Augustine himself says in Book X of the *Confessions*, however, let me first set before you an image of sexuality that pictures it in something like Augustine's way — as having a particular good or purpose, which good we might easily separate from the pleasure it gives and come to seek the pleasure alone.

In *Out of the Silent Planet,* the first of C. S. Lewis's space fantasies, the protagonist Ransom finds himself on the planet of Malacandra, where three species of *hnau* — *sorns*, *pfifltriggi*, and *hrossa* — live together in peace under the rule of Maleldil. In order to learn more about Malacandra, Ransom spends time talking with Hyoi, one of the *hrossa*. The conversation leads at one point to continuation of the species. Is there ever danger on Malacandra that the population of *hrossa* might outstrip food production? The question is almost unintelligible to Hyoi. He cannot understand why they would produce that many offspring.

> Ransom found this difficult. At last he said:
> "Is the begetting of young not a pleasure among the *hrossa?*"
> "A very great one, *Hman.* This is what we call love."
> "If a thing is a pleasure, a *hman* wants it again. He might want the pleasure more often than the number of young that could be fed."

> It took Hyoi a long time to get the point.
>
> "You mean," he said slowly, "that he might do it not only in one or two years of his life but again?"
>
> "Yes."
>
> "But why? Would he want his dinner all day or want to sleep after he had slept? I do not understand."
>
> "But a dinner comes every day. This love, you say, comes only once while the *hross* lives?"
>
> "But it takes his whole life. When he is young he has to look for his mate; and then he has to court her; then he begets young; then he rears them; then he remembers all this, and boils it inside him and makes it into poems and wisdom."
>
> "But the pleasure he must be content only to remember?"
>
> "That is like saying, 'My food I must be content to eat.' "[2]

Augustine's "food as medicine" theory lies very near at hand here, and perhaps it has some plausibility when set in Malacandra. In *Mere Christianity,* however, Lewis applied this kind of thinking very specifically to the matter of sexual morality — not on Malacandra but on earth, the "silent planet."

> You can get a large audience together for a strip-tease act — that is, to watch a girl undress on the stage. Now suppose you came to a country where you could fill a theatre by simply bringing a covered plate on to the stage and then slowly lifting the cover so as to let every one see, just before the lights went out, that it contained a mutton chop or a bit of bacon, would you not think that in that country something had gone wrong with the appetite for food? And would not anyone who had grown up in a different world think there was something equally . . . [odd] about the state of the sex instinct among us?[3]

We can by now make the connections and the argument for ourselves, and I may as well note that in doing so we have reconstructed on our own what is essentially the Roman Catholic argument against contraception. Not long ago, in a different setting, I heard a Catholic theologian put the point almost this way. Contraceptive intercourse is an attempt to separate the pleasure from the good — the pleasure of sexuality from the good of sexuality — and it is

2. C. S. Lewis, *Out of the Silent Planet* (New York: Macmillan, 1965), 72f.
3. C. S. Lewis, *Mere Christianity* (New York: Macmillan, 1960), 75.

therefore a form of autoeroticism. Thus we could say: As nourishment constitutes the good of food, the eating of which incidentally gives pleasure, so also children constitute the good of sexuality, the experience of which incidentally gives pleasure. As we should not grasp for the pleasure of eating apart from the good purpose to which it is divinely ordered, so also we should not seek the pleasure of the sexual act apart from the good to which it is divinely ordered. Food is medicine — that is, its purpose is our sustenance and health. Sexual intercourse sustains not the individual but the species — its purpose is offspring.

Now, to be sure, I think Augustine is wrong about food. It serves, I think, more than one good in human life. It quite properly gives not only nourishment but also enjoyment. And, hence, there should be place in life not only for the banana but also for the banana split. These goods need not conflict — though they may, of course. Too many banana splits may endanger the good of health that food also serves.

For similar reasons I think that the Catholic theologian to whose comment I referred was wrong. Sexual intercourse serves more than one good. It builds up the species through procreation; it also builds up the mutual love of spouses — who, to make the alternative case briskly, when they engage in contraceptive intercourse may be seeking not the pleasure of sex apart from the good of children, but the good of nourishment of their mutual love.

Nevertheless — and, please, do not suppose that I have forgotten that my assignment is to contemplate the renunciations of the devil's ways to which we today may be called — the Catholic argument ought to give us pause. I responded to it by suggesting that in contraceptive intercourse spouses seek one of the several goods of marriage — mutual love, and not a child. But surely, a Catholic interlocutor might reply, we live in a world in which it is also possible to seek a child apart from the relation of mutual love. We can manage that in a laboratory, or even, sometimes, just with the aid of a turkey baster — a thought-provoking rejoinder. I am not for the moment concerned to try to give a full assessment of the morality of assisted reproduction, as we now call it. If it is morally questionable, as I think it is, that is not because it seeks only one of the goods of marriage. That is because of what it means for the identity of the child, who becomes through it our product and project — no longer quite a gift. In this way the Catholic interlocutor can, I think, be satisfactorily answered.

But the argument that I have drawn out of Augustine and Lewis, though it will not, in my judgment, work in quite the way Catholic moral theology has traditionally used it, points us to something very important. What our culture has lost, what our churches have largely lost, what we ourselves may sometimes have lost, is an understanding of the sexual relationship as more than a personally fulfilling undertaking intended to make us happy. The notion that sexuality is a profound but very private and personal form of play is one of Satan's most powerful temptations in our world. It will grip each of us in different ways, and there is, therefore, no cookbook recipe for overcoming this temptation. Fundamentally, however, we must recapture the sense that in the exercise of our sexuality God sets before us a task. It is the task of begetting and rearing children. It is also the task of giving ourselves to our spouse, learning to love that other person as much as we love ourselves, learning to think of ourselves as forever dependent upon that other person and no longer independent or autonomous.

To take that vision of sexuality seriously is to call for a good bit of renunciation in our lives. I have no desire here to engage in a casuistry that attempts to describe how this renunciation must take shape in each and every person's life. Indeed, that cannot be done. The possibilities are many, and we should be able to find the ones that best fit our condition. A culture that encourages people to marry late after they have developed their own independent identities and perhaps have cohabited for a time invites disastrous misunderstandings of marriage. Even the now-common desire of couples to compose their own marriage vows suggests that marriage is our private project designed to serve whatever purposes we give it.[4] The fact that one's spouse no longer makes one happy has become a seemingly compelling reason for divorce. The idea that one must have a child or children "of one's own" gets the point of offspring exactly wrong — and misses, surely, the inner meaning of infant baptism. Indeed, the very idea — with which we are so reluctant to disagree — that sexuality must be affirmed rather than disciplined, ordered, and even suppressed is an idea that opens us wide to very

---

4. David Blankenhorn, "I Do?" *First Things* 77 (November 1997): 14f.

powerful currents of temptation. Troops of grade-school children rushing off to see — more than once — Kate Winslet naked in "Titanic" and learning that love is its own law suggests what powerful currents these are. Against which must be set the greater nobility of discipline, fertility, fidelity. There will be plenty of room here for renunciation.

The Lust of the Eyes

If Augustine's reading of "lust of the flesh" directs our attention to very down-to-earth, bodily temptations, his reading of "lust of the eyes" is concerned with what are, in one sense, more spiritual temptations. They take their root in the restless capacities of the human spirit, its natural inclination to wonder. In particular, Augustine fears "a kind of empty longing and curiosity" that Satan may use to fashion his chains ever more securely around us (X, 35). Much earlier in the *Confessions* Augustine had, in fact, given his readers an example of such vain longing in the depiction of his good friend Alypius, who was for a time sucked into "the empty enthusiasm for shows in the Circus" (VI, 7), carried away "with a most incredible passion, by the gladiatorial shows" (VI, 8). In Book X, however, Augustine is more concerned to take stock of his own temptations, of the "enormous forest, so full of snares and dangers," in which he finds himself (X, 35). His discussion of the many curiosities that entice him away from wholehearted love of God is oft-cited, though just as often bemoaned or criticized.

He is himself no longer carried away by the theater, and he has broken free from the kind of craving that astrological speculation once evoked in him. Nevertheless, there are many small occasions in life when he frequently slips. "I no longer go to the Games to see a dog coursing a hare; but if I happen to be going through the country and see this sport going on, it may attract my attention away from some serious meditation — not so much as to make me turn my horse's body out of the way, but enough to alter the inclination of my mind" (X, 35). Sometimes while sitting at home he suddenly realizes that his attention has been wholly absorbed in "a lizard catching flies or . . . a spider entangling them in his web" (X, 35). He knows these are minor "slips," yet he takes them seriously.

Augustine has, as I noted, often been faulted for this excessively scrupulous examination of conscience in Book X. Robert O'Connell, a noted scholar, nicely states the criticism.

> That examination of conscience makes, surely, some of the most depressing reading in all of Christian literature. There is something profoundly saddening about the portrait it presents: the great Bishop of Hippo tormenting himself about the pleasure he cannot avoid while eating . . . or listening to psalmody . . . ; or berating himself that the spectacle of a dog chasing a hare, or of a lizard snaring a fly, can still distract his interest. . . . Even more saddening, perhaps, the thought of Christian generations who have been confused and troubled by the dreadful indictment of those wholesome human things, to say nothing of Christians today and tomorrow who, influenced by pages like these and others following their inspiration, will continue to doubt their own healthy acceptance of the world God made "good," indeed, "very good."[5]

That there is something to this I have already granted. The renunciations Augustine thought necessary for himself are not necessarily paradigmatic for us, and sometimes his understanding of the created goods of human life is too restrictive. That said, however, there is more here than O'Connell allows. From the world that God made " 'good,' indeed, 'very good,' " we have made the world of 1 John 2. Of it we must say, "Do not love the world or the things in the world." Over it Satan rules. Renunciation is required.

Augustine sees this. He will not allow us to ignore it. For just that reason he is always to be taken seriously. Bonhoeffer is famous for having wondered whether Christians might need to learn to live in the world as if there were no God — *etsi deus non daretur*.[6] I have no idea what he meant by that, and perhaps he himself was not entirely clear. Insofar, though, as it has suggested to some a kind of immersion in the world and its sufferings, we may find in Augustine a better guide. The affirmation of God's world that is required of us demands, by its very nature, a simultaneous renunciation of the world *we* are con-

5. Robert J. O'Connell, *St. Augustine's Confessions: The Odyssey of a Soul* (Cambridge, MA: Harvard University Press, 1969), 133.

6. Dietrich Bonhoeffer, *Letters and Papers From Prison,* enlarged edition, ed. Eberhard Bethge (New York: Macmillan, 1972), 360.

stantly fashioning — in order that it may truly be *God's* world that we affirm.

Our problem is not how to live as if there were no God, how to live with a sense of God's absence, simply loving the neighbor. Our problem is — as was Augustine's — how to love God. How to fix the heart on God. How to love God when immersed in worldliness. And there is no way to do this that does not involve renunciation. Precisely because this world, however corrupted, is good — indeed, very good — because it is God's creation, its ways are bound to be enticing. Our eyes are bound to be drawn — regularly and attentively — to its curiosities and delights. It may be hard to remember that they are *created* goods. When Augustine worries lest he be carried away by "lust of the eyes," he has in mind a dispersal of energy and diffusion of attention — the "empty longing and curiosity" that overwhelms our powers of attention and leaves no place for God.

Might this be an apt characterization of our world — and of us? The number of television programs I can enjoy — given the number of channels now available — is almost endless. The number of magazines — good magazines — I can read is very large. Detective stories proliferate without end. Baseball and football, football and basketball, basketball and baseball seasons overlap seamlessly throughout the year. Indeed, the NCAA basketball tournament now grows so large that every year it dominates the season of Lent. I can now watch a movie at home whenever I want, not just when I happen to go to the theater. For those suitably skilled, the internet and video games offer diversions almost without end. There are shopping centers so large that one can spend a family vacation there. And, of course, I can descend from these heights into the depths: Geraldo as a purportedly serious public affairs commentator might claim some of our attention; the pathos of people willing to say almost anything about themselves and assured of a television audience when they do. Again, I note only a random sample of spectacles that might engross us. I do not undertake the casuistry needed to order properly all these goods in a life directed to God. The issue is not, for the moment, whether these are good gifts of the Creator. Many surely are. How could we suppose that baseball was not? The issue is whether our attention is overwhelmed by an empty longing to know and experience. Here again, there is no recipe, no one answer that fits all.

"But what does it profit a man," Kierkegaard writes, "if he goes further and further and it must be said of him: he never stops going further; when it also must be said of him: there was nothing that made him pause? For pausing is not a sluggish repose. Pausing is also movement. It is the inward movement of the heart."[7] In the midst of a world of good things, proper objects of delight, the devil does not find it hard to enchant the heart and capture the attention. God makes it almost too easy for him, since we can so readily become slaves to what is good. Still, it cannot be entirely wrong to pause and marvel at the wonders of such a world — even at a spider entangling flies in its web. Augustine is not an unerring guide here; yet he was surely right to see that we do not often or regularly manage to love the world as *God's* world. We are not wrong to attend to its delights, but, nonetheless, that pause of attention is not the rest for which the heart longs. It is, at best, a station on life's way. And so, a kind of austerity of the spirit is required, a turning not just from evil but even from what is good — from what is good to the One who is Goodness itself. That turn the devil opposes, and it is therefore needed daily if we are to take up the new identity given us in baptism.

The Pride of Life

I began by noting the Small Catechism's teaching that baptism delivers us from death and the devil. St. Paul is, if anything, even stronger in his claim that the one who has been buried with Christ by baptism is "no longer enslaved to sin" (Rom. 6:6). Nevertheless, Paul can also, in the very same context, put the new life with Christ into future tense: "If we have died with Christ, we believe that we shall also live with him." And Luther could likewise exhort the one who had been delivered from the devil to drown the sinful self daily so that the new man could daily rise with Christ.

This takes us at once into a deep mystery of the Christian life, and Augustine pays it heed under the category of "the pride of life." In Book X, we may recall, Augustine is taking stock of how well he is doing in his new identity as Christian. The conversion in the garden does not mean that the devil's ways no longer tempt him. Hence, he has had to worry about the lust of the flesh and of the eyes. He has

---

7. Søren Kierkegaard, *Purity of Heart Is to Will One Thing* (New York: Harper Torchbooks, 1956), 217f.

had to consider the degree to which he has truly renounced the devil's
ways.

Now, though, he comes to the deepest puzzle when he contem-
plates his desire to be praised by others. "But tell me, Lord, . . . has
this third kind of temptation disappeared from me, or can it ever entirely disappear in this life?" (X, 36) Notice Augustine's problem.
With the temptations that he has grouped under the lust of the flesh,
it is generally possible for Augustine to test himself, to make some es-
timate of how he is doing. If he seems too drawn to food, he can fast.
If he is too much drawn to the love of a woman, he can renounce such
pleasures. He can do without in order to determine whether his heart
is really free for the love of God. With those temptations described as
"lust of the eyes" he also knows how to test his progress. He can give
up certain forms of that empty longing to know, as he gave up magic
and astrology. He can cultivate a self-awareness that makes him alert
to the ways in which his attention is constantly drawn by the surfeit of
wonders in our world. If he sometimes still falls, he can at least rise
quickly and redirect his attention to God.

But what of the pride of life? Can he do without praise from others? When his achievements are praised by others, does he refer that
praise back to God or does he, however subtly, regard it as properly
his own? In this matter he can think of no way to test the sincerity of
his love for God. He could give up wealth or high position, but then,
of course, others might praise him for doing so. Shall he try to live a
bad life so that no one will praise him? That hardly seems right. There
is, he concludes, no satisfactory way to determine how deeply captive
he may still be to the need for praise. "It still tempts me even when I
condemn it in myself; indeed it tempts me even in the very act of condemning it . . ." (X, 38). Augustine hopes that much of the time his
desire for praise is rightly ordered within his love for God. "But
whether this is really how I do feel I do not know. In this matter I
know less of myself than of you" (X, 37).

We cannot fully know ourselves or the sincerity of our own hearts.
So deep and convoluted is what Augustine calls memory, so hidden the
inner recesses of the self, that we cannot plumb its depths. The mind "is
not large enough to contain itself" (X, 8). And to think that we and our
contemporaries often take refuge in the language of sincerity and au-
thenticity. If we are unsure about the rightness of what we do, we have
at least been true to ourselves — and therein, we suppose, lies our no-

bility. Augustine unmasks such pretension by showing how impossible it is to know that we act authentically. "For *Thou, Lord, dost judge me;* because, although *no man knoweth the things of a man, but the spirit of a man which is in him,* yet there is still something of man which even the spirit of man that is in him does not know. But you, Lord, know all of him, you who made him. . . . So I will confess what I know of myself, and I will also confess what I do not know of myself . . ." (X, 5).

Taking Augustine seriously, we might, of course, conclude that this essay — and its assigned topic — lead in a mistaken direction, encouraging us to suppose that we could really know the devil's ways among us and know something of how we ourselves are tempted. Perhaps we shouldn't even try. Such a conclusion would be far too easy, however. There are people who need such advice, who need to be set free from constant self-examination and over-scrupulosity. They need, with Augustine, to reclaim their baptism by learning to hand themselves over to the One who knows them better than they know themselves, by confessing what they know and what they do not know of themselves — and letting it go at that. But only one who has undertaken as serious an examination of conscience as Augustine's is well-positioned to receive such advice, and not all of us will have made it quite that far.

I want, instead, to let Augustine's bewilderment about our ability to know ourselves lead us in a different direction — but toward something equally puzzling about the devil's ways among us. Let me not, says the psalmist, keep company with evildoers (141:4), a request we regularly make our own in Evening Prayer. Indeed, the psalmist quite acutely adds, "and let me not eat of their dainties." And about this I think we may say, very much in the spirit of Augustine's uncertainty about his love of praise, that we don't quite know how to do it or when we are doing it as we should. It will not work to take refuge, as we are surely tempted to, in the truth that we are all evildoers. Travel that road far enough in this context and you arrive not at acceptance of the evildoer but at indifference toward the evil deed. By all means we must make our own confession of evildoing regularly and seriously, but there are evildoers with whom we ought not keep company.

We could think of this as a problem for ecclesiastical life, an ecumenical concern, and it might be good if we were to do so. Speaking only for myself, I confess that I cannot comprehend how churchly discussions of the kinds of difference that can coexist within a "reconciled diversity" can concern themselves more with the necessity of bishops than with the normative meaning of our creation as male and female or the dismembering of infants in the womb. In ecclesiastical life also we must ask for the courage not to company with evildoers. To be sure, it will be hard to know how to do this and how to determine what constitutes such companying, but it cannot be done at all without a simple determination to attempt obedience.

I am, for the moment, however, even more puzzled by how we are to do this in our day-to-day life. Indeed, I don't know how to do it. Sometimes we must company with evildoers as we work on joint projects. How many conversations has your life involved in which you were forced to decide whether this was a moment when you had to speak up? Or whether it was a time to pass? Can you say whether you decided rightly? Can you even honestly say that you know yourself so deeply that you are sure you really tried to decide rightly? Must you speak up on behalf of every lost cause? I shouldn't think so. Must you make yourself obnoxious in doing so? I shouldn't think so. "And so," writes Augustine, "because there are certain positions in human society where the holder of office must be loved and feared by men, the enemy of our true happiness is always close upon us, setting his snares everywhere in the words 'Well done, well done,' and hoping that, while we greedily snatch at them, we shall be taken unawares, shall no longer plan our joy in your truth but shall entrust it to the deceitfulness of men, and shall want to be loved and feared not because of you but instead of you" (X, 36). Here again a certain kind of renunciation is demanded. When and where precisely it is hard to say or know for sure, but it is obedience to which we are called.

What Does Baptism Give or Profit?

I trust it is by now clear that I have attempted nothing very original in this examination of the devil's ways among us. I have had recourse to a venerable threefold classification. Renouncing the devil and his ways calls for chastity, poverty, obedience. In a world where sexuality is chiefly a matter of personal play and fulfillment, we are called to take up marriage as a task set before us by God — the renunciation that is chastity. In a world where a surfeit of delights constantly overwhelms our attentiveness to God, we are called to an austerity of the spirit — the renunciation that is poverty. In a world where we can always find noble and praiseworthy reasons for cooperating with evildoers, we are called to be set apart — the renunciation that is obedience. When baptism delivers from the devil's ways, it does that. In placing the sign of the cross upon mind and heart, it commits us to a life marked by these three renunciations — not for their own sake, to be sure, but to keep the heart fixed on God, whom we are to love with an undivided spirit.

It may be, in fact, that not just we but our entire civilization requires a kind of long purgation of the sort G. K. Chesterton described in his biography of St. Francis.[8] It is well known that Chesterton seldom did any research before writing, and one does not therefore turn to him if one simply wants the most accurate set of facts. At the same time, however, Chesterton had a remarkable ability to grasp the heart of a matter. And in writing about St. Francis, he noted how strange it must seem to us that the same man who could delight in the world and intercede on behalf of the birds, the man so often pictured with his arms uplifted in praise, should also undertake the most ascetic kinds of renunciation. In order to understand this, Chesterton believed, we have to think about the world in which Francis appeared and what its history had been.

St. Francis was born into a world emerging from what we have called the Dark Ages, into a time that saw "a fresh flowering of culture and the creative arts after a long spell of much sterner and even more sterile experience" (34). And the end of the Dark Ages was, Chesterton says, not the end merely of a superstitious time, but "the end of a penance; or, if it be preferred, a purgation."

> It marked the moment when a certain spiritual expiation had been finally worked out and certain spiritual diseases had been finally expelled from the system. They had been expelled by an era of asceticism, which was the only thing that could have expelled them. Christianity had entered the world to cure the world; and she had cured it in the only way in which it could be cured. (36)

Christians could purge the pagan world in which they found themselves not by affirmation but by renunciation. Everything natural had been distorted and perverted, and in those circumstances one

---

8. Gilbert K. Chesterton, *St. Francis of Assisi* (New York: George H. Doran Company, 1924). References will be given by page number in parentheses within the body of the text.

could not preach a religion of affirmation of the natural world. "They knew," Chesterton writes of medieval Christians, "much better than we do what was the matter with them and what sort of demons at once tempted and tormented them; and they wrote across that great space of history the text: 'This sort goeth not out but by prayer and fasting'" (44).

In such a world, a world cleansed by a centuries-long austerity of the spirit, St. Francis appeared. And he found, at last, a world that could be affirmed.

> For water itself has been washed. Fire itself has been purified as by fire. Water is no longer that water into which slaves were flung to feed the fishes. Fire is no longer that fire through which children were passed to Moloch. Flowers smell no more of the forgotten garlands gathered in the garden of Priapus; stars stand no more as signs of the far frigidity of gods as cold as those cold fires. They are all like things newly made and awaiting new names, from one who shall come to name them. Neither the universe nor the earth have now any longer the old sinister significance of the world. They await a new reconciliation with man, but they are already capable of being reconciled. Man has stripped from his soul the last rag of nature-worship, and can return to nature.
>
> While it was yet twilight a figure appeared silently and suddenly on a little hill above the city, dark against the fading darkness. For it was the end of a long and stern night, a night of vigil, not unvisited by stars. He stood with his hands lifted, as in so many statues and pictures, and about him was a burst of birds singing; and behind him was the break of day. (51f.)

I find myself wondering how we should think of the moment in which we stand. It is an important question for us to ask ourselves; for the nature of our historical location tells us much about the task before us. Could it be that we find ourselves at a moment when the church's mission to the world needs once again another period — perhaps a centuries-long period — of purgation? And, therefore, that all those of us who have enjoyed picturing ourselves as Francis, with arms uplifted affirming the creation, ought rather to get down and roll in the snow with him?

It is true, of course, that one and the same struggle faces Christians in every moment of history. The dialectic of enjoyment and renunciation is always essential to Christian living. But in order to know which pole of the dialectic needs emphasizing, we must decide whether we stand with St. Francis in a world that has been cleansed of its demons — or whether we stand somewhat closer to St. Augustine in a world that is just beginning once again that long, austere, cleansing, purifying struggle. In letting Augustine shape my reflections, I may only have been reverting to the book that seems to me the single most powerful piece of Christian writing that I have ever read. But I may also have been suggesting something about the time and place in which we stand, and the renunciations to which Christians will soon be called — if they are not already.

However serious we are about this, and however earnestly we struggle not to love the world or the things of the world, we will surely often fail. It is, after all, as Augustine says, "one thing to get up quickly and another thing not to fall down" (X, 35). We will be part of the very world we must renounce. It is, therefore, good news indeed that God loved this world and gave his only Son not to condemn but to save it (John 3:16-17). Baptism works forgiveness of sins — which forgiveness is, in all its inexplicability, God's way among us, for the sake of which we must be ready to renounce the devil's ways.

As the baptized we are daily to reject those ways and to pray for the strength to learn to love God and his ways. "Give what you command, and command what you will." These words become a kind of throbbing refrain, torn from Augustine's soul, in Book X of the *Confessions*. "Give what you command, and command what you will." And it was these words, Peter Brown writes, that so shocked Pelagius — suggesting, as they do, that the Christian life is not just a matter of our own serious effort.[9] The believer walks in continual peril. We can never fully uncover the depths of our own heart nor suppose that our good intentions suffice. The last renunciation required, therefore, is renunciation of hope in our own power. And hence, on the Fifth Sunday of Easter, having been baptized into Christ's death and resurrection, the church prays in words that are an echo of Augustine's: "O God, form the minds of your faithful people into a single will. Make us love what you command and desire what you promise, that, amid all the changes of this world, our hearts may be fixed where true joy is found."

---

9. Peter Brown, *Augustine of Hippo: A Biography* (Berkeley and Los Angeles: University of California Press, 1969), 177ff.

Powers in Conflict:
Christ and the Devil

CARL E. BRAATEN

Introduction

"Be sober, be watchful. Your adversary the devil prowls around like a roaring lion, seeking someone to devour" (1 Peter 5:8). "The devil" is one of those terms in the Bible that many modern theologians have tried to strike from serious Christian discourse. And yet the word survives in our ordinary language, in statements and phrases like:

— "The devil is in the details."
— "Between the devil and the deep blue sea."
— "Speaking of the devil . . ."
— "The devil made me do it."
— "The devil take the hindmost . . ."
— "He has a devil-may-care attitude . . ."

From these and a hundred other similar aphorisms, one would hardly suspect that the concept of the devil had fallen on hard times. The idea that there exists a negative personal agent at the heart of radical evil, effectively active in all dimensions within and upon human experience, is widely considered a relic of antiquated mythology that no one believes anymore — except for those awful fundamentalists.

I recall an embarrassing incident that happened some years ago. I preached a sermon in our seminary chapel on a Gospel story of Jesus' encounter with the power of the devil. I took its theme to be, one that I reiterated many times: The devil may be strong, but Jesus is even stronger. After chapel my demythologizing Bultmannian New Testament colleague came alongside me on the way to coffee and asked me point blank: Do you really believe in the Devil? Well, that was no place to have a knock-down-and-drag-out fight on the existence of the Devil or the problem of demythologizing. I can't remember what I answered, only the awkwardness of the moment. Later while scanning the universe in the middle of the night I recalled something Paul Tillich once related. After Tillich had published his famous article on "The Concept of the Demonic and Its Significance for Systematic Theology,"[1] something liberal Protestantism had wiped from the slate, Tillich said that Bultmann expressed surprise that he would drag out of the closet such an outmoded piece of mythology.

Liberal Protestants, and now also some progressive Catholics, want to present the Christian faith without causing offense to the modern world, and so the Devil must go. As Peter Berger put it, it is simply "naughty to believe in the Devil."[2] Schleiermacher did his best to eliminate belief in the Devil. Certainly, he conceded, Jesus referred to the Devil from time to time, but only in an offhand manner, and then only to accommodate himself to the superstitious way people talked in those days. The assumption is that Jesus must have known better, otherwise he would not meet the standards of our enlightened age.[3]

We are all familar with various schools of theology that delete from Scripture and tradition any word or belief they find embarrassing or out of phase with current fads and isms. This approach begs the question of what is Christian truth. The Devil has always been part and parcel of the Christian message, first making his appearance in the Old Testament, then entering the New Testament from late Jewish apocalypticism, and ever since he has been an object of serious reflection and speculation among virtually all Christian thinkers, Eastern and Western, Catholic and Protestant, until modern times. Christian

1. Paul Tillich, "Der Begriff des Dämonischen und seine Bedeutung für systematische Theologie," *Theologische Blätter* (Leipzig), V (February 1926): 32-35.
2. Peter Berger, "The Devil and the Pornography of Modern Consciousness," *Worldview* 17 (1974): 35.
3. Schleiermacher's discussion of the Devil appears in his dogmatics, *The Christian Faith*, ed. H. R. Mackintosh and J. S. Stewart (New York: Harper, 1963), 1.1.1.2.

theology must use biblical terms; the Devil, or Satan, or Lucifer are among them. Who would possess the authority to grant us license to remove the Devil from Christian teaching? To rid theology of something so thoroughly anchored in Scripture and the Christian tradition assumes that one can derive Christian truth from some other sources, say, from personal experience or current ideology. But personal experience proves nothing and ideologies come and go with the times. Theology always moves forward in the creative tension between tradition and innovation; we are free to reinterpret the tradition, but not arbitrarily to whack away what we don't like.

I. The Existence of the Devil

True Christianity is stuck with the Devil, like it or not. If believing in the existence of the Devil offends, if it is a stumbling block, that is really not unlike virtually everything else in the Christian system of belief. Any theology that does not take the Devil seriously should not itself be taken seriously. Luther wrote: "It has taken me a long time to discover that it is an article of faith that the Devil is the ruler of this world, the god of this age."[4] An article of faith, to be sure, yet surprisingly the Devil is not mentioned in a single article of the Creed. When the Devil does appear in statements of Synods and Councils, the church is thereby setting limits to dualism within the framework of monotheism, thus rejecting the heresy of believing that two opposing eternal principles exist, the one good, the other evil, as in Manichaeism or Priscillianism. We could say that the Devil is given conditional dogmatic status, with the proviso of always keeping him down to size. Christians should never inflate the Devil's ego. The Devil is not an eternal principle, not infinite, not a co-creator of any kind, but merely a creature, one of the fallen angels, albeit the ring leader. The Fourth Lateran Council (1215 A.D.) taught: "The devil and the other demons were indeed created naturally good by God, but they became evil by their own doing."[5] Otherwise the church's teaching concerning the Devil is to be found chiefly in the writings of the fathers, saints, mystics, and scholastics — a long tradition continued by Luther, Calvin,

4. Martin Luther, "Against the Antinomians," *Luther's Works* 47, pp. 113-114.
5. Quoted in *The Catechism of the Catholic Church*, Part One, p. 98, no. 268.

and Protestant Orthodoxy. It is difficult to reclaim the buried treasure of so rich a tradition, but perhaps we can help a little to roll away the stone.

The first thing we learn is that the decision for or against the existence of the Devil is a decision for or against the integrity of Christianity as such. We simply cannot subtract the Devil, along with demons, angels, principalities, powers, and elemental spirits, without doing violence to the shape of the Christian faith, as transmitted by Scripture and tradition, our primary sources. No room is allowed for these spiritual realities in a strictly materialistic or naturalistic worldview, nor for any other secrets of the Christian mystery, for that matter. "The god of this world has blinded the minds of unbelievers, to keep them from seeing the light of the gospel of the glory of Christ, who is the likeness of God" (2 Cor. 4:4).

Christians ought to be careful — "sober" and "watchful" — about flirting with the assumptions of modern skepticism that call into question belief in the existence or relevance of the Devil, for the same assumptions can go to the jugular of belief in God. Belief in the incarnation and the resurrection of Jesus are equally vulnerable in a secular age — implications that some theologians have not hesitated to draw. The argument that perhaps we may believe in some generalized notion of evil but not in the Devil as a personal agent, with consciousness, intelligence, and will, is likewise dubious, for the same kind of logic is commonly applied to depersonalize God. Both God and the Devil are viewed as projections of the human experience of good and evil, hypostasized symbols of primitive mythology depicting a cosmic struggle between good and evil. Both God and the Devil become unecesssary hypotheses. First the Devil died in the modern world, suffocated by its rationalistic scientism, its atheistic materialism, its nihilistic ideologies; it took a little longer for that to happen to God — and then there were theologians on hand to write the obituary!

By reason alone one can make a strong case for radical evil. Immanuel Kant did, to the chagrin of Goethe and his fellow *philosophes*. Goethe said that by affirming the notion of "radical evil" Kant sullied his philosopher's gown. A world that has produced Hitler, Stalin, Mao Tse Tung, and Pol Pot, a world of genocide, mass starvation, nuclear missiles, and napalm, a society that produces mass killers, serial rapists, and suicide terrorists, may perhaps be ready to believe in the presence of universal and massive evil, natural, moral, and perhaps even metaphyical manifestations of evil, but no one is likely to call this the Devil or Satan apart from his place in the biblical story of salvation. But that is no reason we Christians should play the game of demythologizing and let the Devil slip out of our normal religious discourse.

II. The Devil in Scripture and the Christian Tradition

If we were to paint a picture of the Devil, what would he look like? I called the Devil a "he." Why not a "she"? Strictly because of the weight of tradition. And we hear no voice clamoring for a change. Everyone seems to agree that if we are going to speak of the Devil, the Devil is a "he." Of course, the Devil has no sexual organs, though one of his favorite points of invasion is through the sexual passions of human beings.

More interesting than the question of whether the Devil exists is how the Devil is experienced and represented in the Great Tradition. It makes little sense to worry about whether the Devil is real, if we cannot identify in the actual course of human events those dimensions of experience the Bible attributes to the power of the Devil. The Devil *is* what the Devil *does;* we know the Devil in terms of his actions upon and within individuals and communities.

The profile of the New Testament Devil is rather clearly and consistently drawn. He is the "prince of this world" (John 12:31) and boasts of having all the kingdoms of the earth at his disposal (Matt. 4:9). The Devil is called the "enemy" (Matt. 13:39) and the "evil one" (Matt. 13:19). John calls him the "ruler of this world" (John 12:31; 14:30; 16:11) and Paul the "god of this world" (2 Cor. 4:4). The Devil "was a murderer from the beginning," a "liar and the father of lies" (John 8:44). This means that he claims for himself the honor that belongs to God alone and succeeds in getting people to believe him. The Devil's aim is destruction in both bodily and spiritual terms. All in all, God and the Devil are locked in a cosmic struggle for power and dominion.

To be sure, the chief concern of the New Testament is to tell the good news that in the encounter with Christ the power of the Devil has been checked. The unredeemed who are in bondage to the Devil now have a chance to be liberated. The Devil has met more than his match on the battlefield with Christ. At every decisive point in his life Jesus gets the better of him. In overcoming the temptations of the Devil, Jesus proves who is the stronger. In exorcising demons Jesus demonstrated his superior strength over the servants of Satan. Even in his death on the cross Jesus "disarmed the principalities and powers and made a public example of them, triumphing over them" (Col. 2:15). Paul said that if the rulers of this age had understood what they were up against, they would not have crucified the Lord of glory (1 Cor. 2:8).

But the Devil is still at loose in the world, mortally wounded but still dangerous. His days are numbered, but he continues his treachery, and the Christian community is still vulnerable to the "fiery darts of the evil one" (Eph. 6:16). So the Epistles contain no end of admonitions to withstand "the wiles of the Devil" (Eph. 6:11). In a special way the Christian community is the target of the snares of the Devil. This happens through persecutions from the outside and heresies from the inside. The seductions of Satan come to a head in the work of the Antichrist. And finally, the New Testament promises, the Devil will be cast into a "lake of fire" (Rev. 20:20) and his power will come to an end.

The New Testament picture of the Devil is retained by the early church and the church fathers. The chief fight is against docetists and Marcions. Polycarp spoke for many: "Anyone who does not believe that Jesus Christ is come in the flesh is an antichrist, and anyone who does not believe in the cross's testimony that Jesus really suffered and died, is of the devil," and then he continues in words pertinent to our own day, "anyone who twists Christ's words to suit his own desire and says there is no resurrection or judgment is the first-born child of Satan."[6] Other early fathers are equally attentive to the seductions of Satan within the Christian community. Ignatius was eminently concerned for its order and unity. He "warned the Ephesians to evade the 'stench' of the prince of this world, lest he divert them from the life that Christ wishes for them."[7] All the fathers perceived martyrdom as a struggle of the athletes of Christ against the servants of Satan. The

---

6. Polycarp's Letter to the Church of Philippi, chapter 7. Cited by Jeffrey Burton Russell, *Satan: The Early Christian Tradition* (Ithaca, NY: Cornell University Press, 1981), 42.

7. Russell, *Satan*, 34.

Devil uses torture and death; Christians are to respond by remaining faithful and obedient even unto death.

We could go on to highlight remarkable insights from the fathers on the church's struggles with the Devil in their day. The Middle Ages retained a strong awareness of the presence and power of the Devil, both at the level of popular religiosity and the more erudite speculations of the scholastics. We should go over this ground again to help us reclaim the vivid imagination and sophistication they possessed of the presence of the dark, deadly, and destructive force at work in our souls and society.

We can hardly conclude our brief look at the church's tradition of teaching on the Devil without a word about the revival of Devil-awareness in the Protestant Reformation. This was no doubt largely due to Luther. We could almost say that Luther was full of the Devil, in the sense that no theologian since biblical times was more aware of the Devil's presence and rule over the world than Luther. This may be an embarrassment for many Lutherans today who, like so many other liberal and modern Christians, are just as likely to banish the Devil into oblivion. From Luther's perspective we are living in a time of war; Christians are frontline fighters in a cosmic battle beween God and the Devil. But stronger than his awareness of the Devil's presense was Luther's confidence in the greater power of the gospel. No matter how fierce the Devil is, threatening to devour us, "one little word can fell him." So goes one stanza of Luther's famous hymn, "A Mighty Fortress Is Our God." "No strength of ours can match his might!" But afflicted by a condemning conscience and hit by demons of depression, we can each defiantly say, "I am baptized!" "For God himself fights by our side with weapons of the Spirit" — and for Luther that meant the Word and the Sacraments.

III. Current Manifestations of the Demonic

So as Christians we believe the Devil exists; the full weight of Scripture and the Christian tradition supports that conviction. But that is only half the story. The rest is that we should be keenly aware of the current manfestations of the demonic in our souls, in our communities, and in the wider world around us. If it should ever happen that we enter a "brave new world" from which all evils have been eliminated, the concept of the Devil would surely wither away, no matter how much a part of the sacred record. We need not worry. The horrors of the twentieth century have produced a keen sense of evil beyond church boundaries. Moreover Satanism is alive outside the Christian frame of reference, along with the revival of the occult among counter-culture groups. Elements of Satanism flourish in "heavy metal" and rap groups that extol the demonic values of cruelty, ugliness, violence, rape, suicide, promiscuous sex, all pounded out in deafening sounds. The Devil's noise drowns out the voice of God. "Be still and know that I am God," says the psalmist (Psalm 46:10). The Devil's noise dulls the ability to hear that "still small voice" that Elijah heard (1 Kings 19:12).

Turning on the evening news is like watching a horror film. The Devil's way is hatred and violence, and don't we see a lot of that? We have witnessed the aftermath of World War II on TV, the genocide of Jews and Cambodians, the concentration camps, the ovens and gas chambers, the empty stares of emaciated survivors and the stacks of bones. We have seen the victims of napalm and heard the screams of burning children. The media love to indulge the public with gory accounts of the grisly mass killings of demon-possessed individuals, the likes of Speck, Gacy, Dahmer, Manson, Jones, Cunanon, Kascynski, McVeigh, just to mention a few of the grosser ones taking their turns in the limelight. Psychiatrists have their words to describe these twisted minds. Freud chalked it all up to a death instinct, but Carl Jung said we may as well call it the Devil.[8] The demons never died, he said, they merely became diseases. Why not view the Devil then as the focal point and unifying force that exploits human faults and drives them into destructive and death-dealing orgies? Demon-possession by any other name remains the same.

Tillich defined the demonic as a "structure of destruction." It would be simplistic mythology to think of demons, or the Devil himself, as beings flitting about in the air. We should rather think of them as the spiritual essence of systems and structures gone amuck. Millions of Germans endorsed the ideals of national socialism — national honor, pride of race, full employment, social order. Without them knowing it, the demonic had permeated and poisoned all political

---

8. Jeffrey Burton Russell, *Lucifer: The Devil in the Middle Ages* (Ithaca, NY: Cornell University Press, 1994), 303.

forms and forums, often with the implicit cooperation of the churches, giving rise to the Hitler Youth, the SS, the Gestapo, the ideology of racial purity, and the revival of Norse mythology. And the rest is history. No need to personify demons as little beings in the sky; they are very much down-to-earth, embodied in economic, social, political, military, and ideological structures of destruction. In our society they are powerfully at work in the media, in journalism, in education, in entertainment, in sports, take your pick. You can hardly go to a movie without seeing a pretty face put on fornication, adultery, sodomy, along with the trashing of traditional sexual morality, marital fidelity, and a family structure in which children have a right to know and be loved and raised by both their parents. A society is in dire jeopardy when its families are under siege.

And let's not stop there, but rather go behind the scenes of our great legal, medical, educational, and religious professions, and we'll see how the demonic — chameleon-like — changes its colors according to the circumstances. Those of us in the religious professions are not without sordid examples that keep us aware of the presence and power of the demonic.

The cumulative witness of Scripture and the tradition is that we are presently in a war of cosmic dimensions, whether we like it or not; and it is not a war against flesh and blood but against powers and principalities, to be fought not with guts and guns but with grace and the obedience born of faith. The term "culture wars" does not get to the bottom of it; it is not a war between liberals and conservatives, not between traditionalists and modernists, and not between political parties. The Devil is too cunning and clever for that; for he is always willing to volunteer his services to both sides at once. That is why it is often appropriate to say, "A plague on both your houses."

By what criterion can we tell the difference? The criterion is a matter of life or death. The Devil is the inventor of all those de-words — destruction, decadence, debasement, defilement, deception, defamation, degeneration, desecration, etc. For this reason some theologians have said that the Devil's true being is his lack of being. Dante placed the Devil at the dead center of the earth "with his buttocks stuck in the ice at the dead point of the turning world."[9] At the dead center there is a void, sheer nothingness. The Devil is like a vacuum

---

9. Russell, *Lucifer*, 225-226.

that sucks other beings into the void of his own nonbeing. Whatever the merits of such speculation, the point is well taken that the Devil is the Evil One who wills hatred and violence, destruction and death. Now if we look at our society, where is this most painfully evident? Not only in the crimes of violence that get the big headlines. The Devil is a murderer from the beginning, sucking up the lives of the unborn into the black hole of his own evil empire. One sobering statistic: ninety-nine percent of all murders in the United States are abortions. Add to that a second statistic, in the United States eighty percent of black babies are born outside of marriage, and thirty percent among whites. We have to say this is a devastating time for families and children. Child abuse begins at the beginning, in many cases even before they leave their mother's womb.

IV. Discerning the Spirits

When asked, "Do you believe in the Devil?", the answer must be "No." Believing means to trust, to have confidence in someone. We do not believe in the Devil; we do not believe his lies. But we do believe that we all enter a world bent out of shape, and that the Devil is the source of a magnetic pull toward evil deeply embedded in every individual and the societies in which they live. He works behind our backs drawing us toward evil without our being aware of it. The catechisms of the church's tradition call it "original sin," Satan's black mark upon our souls from the time of conception. Reinhold Niebuhr liked to quote the *London Times:* "The doctrine of original sin is the only empirically verifiable doctrine of the Christian faith."[10] And Karl Barth wrote in his *Romans Commentary,* "Is it not [i.e., original sin] . . . the doctrine which emerges from all honest study of history?"[11] For Christians it is no huge stretch of the imagination to link original sin to the presence of a real personal force actively engaged, with intelligence and will, to corrupt the whole creation and throw it off course.

So Christians are exhorted: "Put on the whole armor of God, that you may be able to stand against the wiles of the devil" (Eph. 6:11). I

10. Reinhold Niebuhr, *Man's Nature and His Communities* (New York: Scribner, 1965), 24.

11. Karl Barth, *The Epistle to the Romans* (New York: Oxford University Press, 1968), 86.

am afraid many of us will shrug our shoulders at this seemingly super-
fluous counsel. We go about our normal routine, get up in the morning, read the paper, walk the dog, send the kids off to school; it is a
sane, civilized world, and the neighbors are really nice. Northfield's
motto says it well: Cows, Colleges, and Contentment! We have no fear
of demons; so we are hardly good candidates for exorcism. We know
lots about lusts, passions, addictions, feelings of worthlessness, depression, anorexia, mental illness, gambling, drugs, AIDS, alcoholism,
overeating, and we go to doctors, counsellors, clinics, and spas for
therapy. As Christians, like everyone else, we need all the help we can
get when we're sick, but perhaps the church, with due caution, should
reclaim the apostolic ministry of exorcism, to deal with the various
obsessions and possessions of its members in modern times. The
church in Africa has not relinquished this aspect of biblical Christianity. But, of course, it cannot afford all the expensive substitutes for the
biblical treatment of demonic possession. Perhaps we ought to reconsider whether our enlightened sophistication has not rendered us
oblivious to the demonic. An old English Puritan, Richard Greenham,
anticipated C. S. Lewis's famous epigram, declaring that "it is the pol-
icy of the Devil to persuade us there is no Devil."[12]

It is true, as Christians we are not to cower in fear and timidity before the forces of evil, the powers and principalities, the structures of
destruction. We now view all things in the light of Christ and his victory. *Christus Victor!* The genuine demythologizing that comes from
the gospel reveals that we are free, really free, not to be in bondage to
the powers under the Devil's dominion. "If God is for us, who is
against us?" cried Paul. "We are more than conquerors through him
[i.e., Christ] who loved us. For I am sure that neither death nor life,
nor angels, nor principalities, nor things present, nor things to come,
nor powers, nor height, nor depth, nor anything else in all creation,
will be able to separate us from the love of God in Christ Jesus our
Lord" (Rom. 8:31a, 37-39).

The rule of Christ is now superior. The crucified and risen Lord is
in charge; he is the ground and goal of the universe, the revealed mystery at the heart of the world. Wherever Christ is preached, the demons are rousted out of hiding, unmasked, and defanged.

---

12. Quoted by Jeffrey Burton Russell, *Mephistopheles: The Devil in the Modern World*
(Ithaca, NY: Cornell University Press, 1986), 80.

It happened that I grew up on the island of Madagascar — synonymous with aepyornis eggs, lemurs, and vanilla sticks. My parents were missionaries. The Malagasy believed in demons, evil spirits, without any coaching from the missionaries. My father did not need to spend a lot of time insisting on the reality of the Devil and demons. There may have been a few missionaries looking for demons behind every bush, but for the most part the message of the missionaries was clear and direct: Christ has triumphed over them! My father would never have dreamed of denying the existence of demons; they were simply the givens of Malagasy religion. But the gospel is the power to deny them free reign, by denouncing them and destroying their deadly power by the preaching of the word. For God in Christ has appeared on earth, has penetrated enemy territory, and shown through his cross and resurrection that he is stronger than all the devils in the world. The victory is certain; yet the battle continues until the Lordship of Christ is acknowledged on all fronts and visible to all. What the missionaries accomplished in Madagascar by their version of "mere Christianity" is a marvellous success story that many pseudo-Christians in America dismiss as an instance of colonialism and imperialism. The idea of preaching Christ to people who are perfectly happy in their own religion! Except, the missionaries knew the Malagasy were not happy, for they lived in constant fear of evil spirits, in bondage to the elemental spirits of the universe.

Now the Devil's dominion, checked by Christ, continues to be limited by the very existence of the church of Christ on earth. The church has been given the gift of spiritual discernment, to see through the deception of the Devil by refusing to chase after the isms that implement his strategies. The church is the community elected by God to exist within the larger community of a nation or culture, whose very presence relativizes every idolatrous claim to ultimacy and questions the legitimacy of every system that does not honor the Lordship of Jesus Christ. In the now famous words of Stanley Hauerwas, "The church does not have a social ethic, she is a social ethic."

This means that the church, which can claim no special powers and privileges before the secular state, is called by God to take a definite stand on whatever concerns the wider human community. The church must simply take a definite stance, whether it is politically expedient, pragmatically realistic, or at high cost to its institutional self-interest. The church may be required to embark on the confessing mode, to be a witness for the truth, whether or not it has any chance of success. Standing up to seductive and menacing powers, whether political or cultural, the church's stance is grounded in its fellowship with Christ, the way, the truth, and the life. When the demonic powers are unmasked by the sheer fact that the confessing church has the courage to take a definite stand, they lose their control over peoples' souls. The three examples of our century are the confessing church in Hitler's Germany, the civil rights movement in the United States, and the struggle against apartheid in South Africa. The spiritual gift of discernment made all the difference, along with the courage to back it up. There was nothing spectacular in any of this, simply the refusal to go along with the powers that be. "Hell no, we won't go," was the chant of the antiwar demonstrators during the Vietnam War. My wife and I were among them. The powers were cut down to size; they shrunk before the eyes of those who would not bow before them in fear and trembling. The early Christians would not lay a pinch of incense at the high altar of almighty Caesar, and in that act of faith and obedience placed dynamite at the pillars of the pagan Empire.

The church's resistance against the god of this age will fail unless the church demonstrates in her own life and fellowship the joy of freedom from its clutches. Just by being the church, in faithful witness and worship, the church is God's instrument to speak truth to power, to bring the rule of the powers into crisis, to place them under judgment. The alternative strategy of the modern church of issuing social statements at every synod assembly that nobody reads or obeys has never caused the powers-that-be to bow down in fear and trembling.

Christ's church, by her presence, preaching, and patterns of life, may become a mighty witness and forceful address beyond her own borders, that those outside the church may tacitly accept the church's wisdom as a benchmark for their own most deeply seated human longings and concerns. Christian or not they may see in the church's witness and life a standard worth reaching for, a model of a good life that finds the right balance between mercy and justice, freedom and order.

As a Christian people we are called to be the church in word and deed, living from the fact that Christ has overcome the power of the Evil One, holding his influence at bay by virtue of this faith. In this sense it falls to the church to take responsibility for the cultural crisis in which we live today.

Conclusion

Under the present conditions where can this sort of thing happen today? Those of us growing up in the Midwest placed a lot of trust in our educational institutions, colleges, and seminaries. Now where can we best train the troops for the struggles ahead? Archbishop Fulton Sheen used to say: "The best way I know to be sure that your children will lose their faith is to send them to a Catholic college." Other denominations are no better off. The churchly substance of the nation's church colleges has become thin. They seem to run from anything distinctively Christian, often including chapel services and religion departments, as from the smell of a skunk. And with the collapse of serious catechetical instruction, a whole generation of Christian youth may be lost to the church. Only a small percentage of young people remain faithful to the church after confirmation.

If I had an answer to the question I've posed here at the end, I'd write a book about it. Christians must ask out of deep concern, how can we get the church moving again in the right direction? We don't have all the answers, but we do know some of the essential ingredients. The first thing is a return to the sources, encouraging faithfulness, and the second is the cause of Christian unity, striving for reconciliation. The two things go together, for true unity must be based on a consensus of faith in the truth of God revealed. This is a modest proposal, yet nothing less will be equal to the magnitude of the task ahead.

I will close these reflections with a prayer taken from E. Gordon Rupp's book, *Principalities and Powers*, his modernized version of an old Cornish prayer:

"From 'Anities and 'Alities
and 'Ologies and 'Isms,
Good Lord, deliver us."[13]

---

13. Quoted by Hendrick Berkhof, *Christ and the Powers*, tr. John H. Yoder (Scottdale, PA: Mennonite Publishing House, 1962), 78-79.

The Gospel of Life Is the Gospel

RICHARD JOHN NEUHAUS

The phrase "culture of death" has, of course, entered current conversations through its repeated use in the 1995 encyclical, *Evangelium Vitae*. As I went back once again to that complex, compelling, and deeply disturbing document, I was impressed as I had not been before that its title, "The Gospel of Life," is much more than a piece of effective moral rhetoric. The encyclical's argument is that the Gospel of life is, quite simply, the Gospel. It follows that the culture of death is much more than a moral aberration producing tragic consequences of vast proportions. The culture of death is the anti-Gospel.

It is commonly said that *Evangelium Vitae* is a moral encyclical dealing with threats to human life, with specific reference to abortion, euthanasia, eugenics, and, although with lesser emphasis, the death penalty. That is true enough, but it is far from adequate. Even less adequate is to say that the encyclical is an exercise in Christian ethics. Ethics is a pale and sickly term having to do with theories of values. While it undoubtedly deals with theories, values, cultural criticism, and much else, *Evangelium Vitae* is an exercise in theology. What it says about morality is not an appendage or implication or even a consequence of theology. It *is* theology. The 1993 encyclical, *Veritatis Splendor* (The Splendor of Truth), is emphatic in asserting that moral theology is *theology* and social doctrine is *doctrine*. In the Church's teaching, the distinction between *kerygma* — the proclamation of the saving Gospel — and *didache* — the instruction for the living of that Gospel — is never a separation. The distinction is not even a bright line. *Kerygma* and *didache* are all of a piece.

Evangelium Vitae asserts that the commandment, "You shall not kill," is integral to the fullness of revelation. "Detached from this wider framework, the commandment is destined to become nothing more than an obligation imposed from without, and very soon we begin to look for its limits and try to find mitigating factors and exceptions. Only when people are open to the fullness of the truth about God, man, and history will the words 'you shall not kill' shine forth once more as a good for man in himself and in his relations with others" (48). Put differently, the moral doctrine of *Evangelium Vitae* is in no way heteronomous. More accurately, it is theonomous, and most accurately it is, in the fullest sense of the term, evangelical. It is not derived from the revelation of God in Christ; it *is* the revelation of God in Christ. That at least is the argument of the encyclical as I understand it, and, if I am right, it is an argument that must be taken with utmost seriousness both by Catholics and by those who are ecumenically engaged with the Catholic Church.

That the Gospel of life is the Gospel itself is evident in several formulations of *Evangelium Vitae* that appeal directly to *Lumen Gentium* (Light to the Nations) section 25, where the Second Vatican Council addresses the infallibility that Christ wills for his Church. It speaks of teaching that "the faithful are to accept and adhere to with a religious assent of soul." *Lumen Gentium* declares: "This is the infallibility which the Roman Pontiff, the head of the college of bishops, enjoys in virtue of his office, when, as the supreme shepherd and teacher of all the faithful, who confirms his brethren in their faith (cf. Luke 22:32), he proclaims by a definitive act some doctrine of faith or morals. . . . For then the Roman Pontiff is not pronouncing judgment as a private person. Rather, as the supreme teacher of the universal Church, as one in whom the charism of the infallibility of the Church herself is individually present, he is expounding or defending a doctrine of Catholic faith."

The Council's teaching is that, when the Church speaks in this authoritative manner, it is not saying something new but is clarifying what has been revealed by God. In the words of *Lumen Gentium:* "When either the Roman Pontiff or the body of bishops together with him defines a judgment, they pronounce it in accord with revelation itself. All are obliged to maintain and be ruled by this revelation, which, as written or preserved by tradition, is transmitted in its entirety through the legitimate succession of bishops and especially through the care of the Roman Pontiff himself. Under the guiding light of the Spirit of truth, revelation is thus religiously preserved and faithfully expounded in the Church."

That *Evangelium Vitae* intends to be such an authoritative exercise of the teaching of the ordinary magisterium is evident in the formulations employed no less than three times; first regarding the taking of innocent human life, and then applying that teaching to abortion and euthanasia. (It is noteworthy that such a formulation is not used with respect to condemning capital punishment, although on that question the encyclical clearly indicates a development of doctrine which may someday eventuate in such an authoritative definition.) With regard to the meaning of the commandment "You shall not kill," section 56 of *Evangelium Vitae* declares: "Therefore, by the authority which Christ conferred upon Peter and his successors, and in communion with the bishops of the Catholic Church, *I confirm that the direct and voluntary killing of an innocent human being is always gravely immoral.* This doctrine, based upon that unwritten law which man, in the light of reason, finds in his own heart (cf. Romans 2:14-15), is reaffirmed by Sacred Scripture, transmitted by the tradition of the Church, and taught by the ordinary and universal magisterium." Employing the same formula, it is later said, "*I declare that direct abortion, that is, abortion willed as an end or as a means, always constitutes a grave moral disorder,* since it is the deliberate killing of an innocent human being" (62). And then a third time, "*I confirm that euthanasia is a grave violation of the law of God,* since it is the deliberate and morally unacceptable killing of a human person" (65).

This, then, is the authoritative status of the Church's teaching on abortion and euthanasia. The encyclical relates that teaching also to reproductive technologies, embryo experimentation, and other practices, all of which are discussed in considerable detail. It is in the nature of Catholic teaching, and it is especially evident in this pontificate, that the Church, in addition to requiring assent in obedience to authority, seeks to elicit assent through persuasive argument. Such persuasion is required by respect for the dignity of free and reasonable persons. While *Evangelium Vitae* surely intends to pronounce the truth, the form of the document is not that of a pronunciamento but of an extended argument and meditation on the meaning of the Gospel. The argument as addressed to Christians is that the moral truth of the Gospel of life is indeed the Gospel itself. The argument as addressed to "all people of good will" is that the moral conclusions of the encyclical are both vindicated by clear reason and essential to a humane and just society. It is to the first argument, that having to do with the meaning of the Gospel, that I will chiefly attend in this paper.

The claim of *Evangelium Vitae* is that, in addressing questions such as abortion and euthanasia, the Gospel itself is at stake. Were that not the case, the consciences of the faithful would not be bound by the Church's teaching authority. The doctrine expounded by the encyclical is, to use a favored phrase of Joseph Cardinal Ratzinger, part of "the structure of faith." Ecumenically-minded Christians who do not hold themselves to be obliged by the magisterium of the Catholic Church must nonetheless be impressed by the solemn weight the Church attaches to this teaching. The more fruitful engagement for our present purposes, however, is not with the authority by which the doctrine is taught but with the doctrine itself. *Evangelium Vitae* is a document of almost fifty thousand words and presents an argument of many parts. I will here only be able to flag, as it were, the shape of the argument, and will then return to the "culture of death" as the anti-Gospel.

The very first sentence of the encyclical asserts, "The Gospel of life is at the heart of Jesus' message." It goes on to say that this Gospel "is to be preached with dauntless fidelity as 'good news' to the people of every age and culture." The angel's announcement to the shepherds of "good news of a great joy" is about the birth of Christ, but it also "reveals the full meaning of every human birth . . . the foundation and fulfillment of joy at every child born into the world." The heart of the Messiah's "redemptive mission" is in his words, "I came that they may have life, and have it abundantly" (1). While Jesus is speaking of eternal life in communion with God, our bodily life in time "is the fundamental condition, the initial stage and an integral part of the entire unified process of human existence." To deny bodily life in time is to deny the process by which human life, "unexpectedly and undeservedly" — that is, by grace — "far exceeds the dimensions of [this] earthly existence." While life on earth is not an "ultimate" but a "penultimate" reality, the penultimate participates in the ultimate and has "sacred value." This sacred value is attested to by "the light of reason and the hidden action of grace" as well as by "the natural law written in the heart." For Christians, "the incomparable value of every human person" is most powerfully declared in the fact that "God so loved the world that he gave his only Son." Thus the proposition follows: "The Gospel of God's love for man, the Gospel of the dignity of the person, and the Gospel of life are a single and indivisible Gospel" (2).

Vatican II is cited: "By his incarnation the Son of God has united himself in some fashion with every human being." "Therefore," says *Evangelium Vitae*, "every threat to human dignity and life" strikes at the "core of [the Church's] faith in the redemptive incarnation of the Son of God" (3). Much later in the argument, we read: "The Gospel of life is not simply a reflection, however new and profound, on human life. Nor is it merely a commandment aimed at raising awareness and bringing about significant changes in society. Still less is it an illusory promise of a better future. The Gospel of life is something concrete and personal, for it consists in the proclamation of the very person of Jesus" (29). The very person of Jesus is made vulnerable in every human being.

Father Avery Dulles has aptly described the thinking of John Paul II as "prophetic humanism." *Evangelium Vitae* radiates a passion for the human project, and God's incarnational investment in that project. Psalm 8 is quoted: "What is man that you are mindful of him, and the son of man that you care for him? . . . Yet you have made him little less than a god, and crown him with glory and honor." "The glory of God shines on the face of man," says the encyclical, and St. Ambrose is invoked to stir our wonder at that glory. In man the Creator finds his rest, Ambrose wrote.

> The sixth day is finished and the creation of the world ends with the formation of that masterpiece which is man, who exercises dominion over all living creatures and is as it were the crown of the universe and the supreme beauty of every created being. Truly we should maintain a reverential silence, since the Lord rested from every work he had undertaken in the world. He rested then in the depths of man, he rested in man's mind and in his thought, for he had created man endowed with reason, capable of imitating him, of emulating his virtue, of hungering for heavenly graces. . . . I thank the Lord our God who has created so wonderful a work in which to take his rest. (35)

This elevated view of man might in some Christian circles today be criticized as anthropocentric, but it is more accurately understood as theocentric and christocentric. It is a doxological response to the glory of God reflected in the human being by virtue of creation, incarnation, and redemption. It is joining in the Creator's delight in his human creature. Irenaeus is repeatedly cited, *Gloria Dei vivens homo* — the glory of God is man fully alive. While sin deformed the image of God and turned man against himself and others (the story of Cain and Abel looms large in the encyclical), the glory is restored by the incarnation, for "Christ is the image of the invisible God" (Col. 1:15) and he "reflects the glory of God and bears the very stamp of his nature" (Heb. 1:3). The life promised and given in Christ "is 'eternal' because it is a full participation in the life of the 'Eternal One' " (36). "Here," we are told, "the Christian truth about life becomes most sublime. The dignity of this life is linked not only to its beginning, to the fact that it comes from God, but also to its final end, to its destiny of fellowship with God." In the light of this truth, Irenaeus completes his praise of man, *Vita autem hominis visio Dei* — the life of man is the vision of God (37). Thus is it evident that human life, every human life, is in its origins and in its end and at every point along the way a project of God.

The bringing into being of a new life is, quite literally, "a divine undertaking" (43). Marriage and family are the "sanctuary of life" and, as such, are ever open to new life. As might be expected, the encyclical includes an extended reflection on the linkage between contraception and abortion, a linkage that is today increasingly recognized also by non-Catholics. The necessary distinctions are made: "Certainly, from the moral point of view contraception and abortion are specifically different evils: The former contradicts the full truth of the sexual act as the proper expression of conjugal love, while the latter destroys the life of a human being; the former is opposed to the virtue of chastity in marriage, the latter is opposed to the virtue of justice and directly violates the divine commandment 'you shall not kill' " (12). Both contraception and abortion betray an instrumental view of "the other," the new life that is a project of God.

If evils such as abortion and euthanasia are so emphatically excluded by God's will for his human creatures, one may wonder why these practices are not explicitly condemned in Scripture. This, says *Evangelium Vitae*, "can easily be explained by the fact that the mere possibility of harming, attacking or actually denying life in these circumstances is completely foreign to the religious and cultural way of thinking of the people of God." Various passages are cited in support of the biblical "certainty that the life which parents transmit has its origins in God." Moreover, in the New Testament, the advent of the Messianic age is revealed by unborn children. Here again St. Ambrose is cited, this time on the meeting between Mary and her cousin Elizabeth: "Elizabeth was the first to hear the voice; but John was the first to experience grace. She heard according to the order of nature; he leaped because of the mystery. She recognized the arrival of Mary; he, the arrival of the Lord. The woman recognized the woman's arrival; the child, that of the child" (45).

The teaching of *Evangelium Vitae* is not to be confused with "vitalism," a worship of the "life force" itself, which is a form of idolatry. "Certainly the life of the body in its earthly state is not an absolute good for the believer, especially as he may be asked to give up his life for a greater good." Here the encyclical lifts up the example of the martyrs who, following Christ, made a gift of their life in service to the truth — a theme that is also powerfully developed in *Veritatis Splendor*. But then it is added, in accord with Christian teaching from the earliest martyrs to the present day: "No one, however, can arbitrarily choose whether to live or die; the absolute master of such a decision is the Creator alone, in whom 'we live and move and have our being' (Acts 17:28)" (47). What we cannot choose for ourselves we cannot choose for others. There is a "law of life" that is not something imposed but inherent in every human being. Because each life is a divine undertaking, there is a good in caring for that life. "The good to be done is not added to life as a burden which weighs on it, since the very purpose of life is that good, and only by doing it can life be built up" (48).

This "law of life," which is God's gracious gift, is completed in Jesus who "does not deny the law but brings it to fulfillment" (Matt. 5:17). The Old Testament prophets forcefully reminded the people of this law of life, and Jesus sums up both the law and the prophets in the rule of mutual love (Matt. 7:12). *Evangelium Vitae* declares, "In Jesus the law becomes once and for all the 'Gospel,' the good news of God's lordship over the world, which brings all life back to its roots and its original purpose." This is what St. Paul means in Romans 8:2 when he speaks of "the law of the Spirit of life in Christ Jesus." The most basic expression of that law, following the example of Christ who gave his life for his friends (John 15:13), is the gift of self in love for others. First John is cited, "We know that we have passed out of death into life because we love the brethren" (1 John 3:14; 49).

The encyclical then turns to Jesus' dialogue with the rich young man in Matthew 19, which, it will be remembered, is a central text also of *Veritatis Splendor*. Jesus' answer to his question, "What must I do to have eternal life?", *Evangelium Vitae* says, is that "this life is attained through the observance of the Lord's commandments, including the commandment 'you shall not kill.'" That, of course, is the first commandment mentioned by Jesus in response to the young man's question. And here we find a succinct summary of my title proposition that the Gospel of life as presented in *Evangelium Vitae* is, in fact, the Gospel itself: "God's commandment is never detached from his love: It is always a gift meant for man's growth and joy. As such, it represents an essential and indispensable aspect of the Gospel, actually becoming 'gospel' itself: joyful good news. The Gospel of life is both a great gift of God and an exacting task for humanity. It gives rise to amazement and gratitude in the person graced with freedom, and it asks to be welcomed, preserved, and esteemed, with a deep sense of responsibility. In giving life to man, God demands that he love, respect, and promote life. The gift thus becomes a commandment, and the commandment is itself a gift" (52).

The Gospel of life, the encyclical contends, is the cohering theme of God's revelation. In the Old Testament, "the people of the covenant, although slowly and with some contradictions," were led toward the truth proclaimed by Jesus that love of God and love of neighbor are inseparable. As he says in Matthew 22, "On these two commandments depend all the law and the prophets." The Church's understanding from the beginning is reflected in the *Didache,* probably written in the first century, that contrasts "The Way of Life" and "The Way of Death" in a manner that parallels *Evangelium Vitae*'s delineation of "the culture of life" and "the culture of death." The encyclical quotes the *Didache*'s contrast of the two people who follow the opposing ways: "There are two ways, a way of life and a way of death; there is a great difference between them. In accordance with the precept 'You shall not kill,' you shall not put a child to death by abortion nor kill it once it is born. The way of death is this: They show no compassion for the poor, they do not suffer with the suffering, they do not acknowledge their Creator, they kill their children and by abortion cause God's creatures to perish; they drive away the needy, oppress the suffering, they are advocates of the rich and unjust judges of the poor; they are filled with every sin" (54).

Toward the end of *Evangelium Vitae* it is asserted that "the law of life" is the Gospel, that the Gospel is nothing less than Jesus Christ, and that all of this is by the grace of God. "Jesus is the only Gospel: We have nothing further to say nor any other witness to bear." Gregory of Nyssa is cited: "Man as a being is of no account; he is dust, grass, vanity. But once he is adopted by the God of the universe as a son, he becomes part of the family of that Being, whose excellence and greatness no one can see, hear, or understand. What words, thoughts or flight of the spirit can praise the superabundance of this grace? Man surpasses his nature: Mortal, he becomes immortal; perishable, he becomes imperishable; fleeting, he becomes eternal; human, he becomes divine" (80).

The argument of *Evangelium Vitae* contains many arguments. Its message is applied in moral judgments about various medical and scientific practices, as well as about the foundations of human rights and democratic society which, when undermined by "the culture of death," lead to the "tyrant state." The case is advanced that the imperative of protecting the vulnerable is evident from natural law and public reason that is available not only to Christians but to all people of good will. There is a pastorally compelling treatment of the difficulties that lead women to procure abortions, of the moral responsibility of men in such circumstances, and of care for women who suffer the consequences of abortion. These and many other subjects are addressed by *Evangelium Vitae*. In this presentation I have limited myself to the simple but utterly critical proposition that the Gospel of life *is* the Gospel.

I believe it is important for us to understand that the teaching of the Catholic Church — a teaching which she believes is attended by infallible authority — is that disagreement about abortion, euthanasia, and the protection of innocent human life is disagreement about the Gospel of Jesus Christ. *Evangelium Vitae* intends to present not simply the moral implications of the Gospel but the Gospel itself. The mindset and practices of "the culture of death" are rooted not simply in moral error but in enmity toward the God of life. This is repeatedly and dramatically underscored by appeal to scriptural texts from Genesis to Revelation. Cain's murder of his brother Abel "is a page rewritten daily . . . in the book of human history" (7). The Lord's question to Cain is addressed to us today, "What have you done?" (10). Cain attempts to excuse himself by evasion and lies, thus following the lead of the Evil One who, as Jesus says, was a liar and a murderer from the beginning (8). Satan deceives us and we end up by calling evil good and good evil, by turning projects of sin and death into rights and benefits (53). The Marian Church, says *Evangelium Vitae*, is the "woman clothed with the sun" of Revelation 12, whose child the dragon would destroy. "Mary helps the Church to realize that life is always at the center of a great struggle between good and evil, between light and darkness." The child of Revelation 12 is a figure of Christ but "also of every person, every child." The Church untiringly proclaims the words of Jesus, "Whoever receives one such child in my name receives me." It follows that "rejection of human life, in whatever form that rejection takes, is a rejection of Christ" (104).

As the woman of the Apocalypse flees for shelter in the desert and finds a place prepared by God, so God, as a sign of his love, has prepared for his people a place of shelter that is also "the place of trial." The angel announced, "Be not afraid, Mary, [for] with God nothing will be impossible." The annunciation to Mary is the annunciation to the Church. In her son and our Lord "the forces of death have already been defeated." The encyclical ends with a triumphant crescendo: "The Lamb who was slain is alive, bearing the marks of his passion in the splendor of the resurrection. He alone is master of all the events of history: He opens its 'seals' (cf. Rev. 5:1-10) and proclaims in time and beyond the power of life over death. In the 'new Jerusalem,' that new world toward which human history is traveling, 'death shall be no more, neither shall there be mourning nor crying nor pain anymore, for the former things have passed away.'" Meanwhile the pilgrim people of life and for life look with confidence to Mary who looks with unfailing trust to "God, the Creator and lover of life" (105).

Today's conflict over abortion, euthanasia, eugenics, and the advancing debasement and destruction of human life is at the heart of the great cultural and political wars that mark our time. It is also a conflict of moral judgments among Christians. In the teaching of the Catholic Church, however, the conflict is about immeasurably more than that. "In the beginning was the Word. . . . In him was life, and the life was the light of men. The light shines in the darkness, and the darkness has not overcome it." What, then, is "the culture of death?" The culture of death is the darkness. It is the darkness that has not, and will not, overcome the light. That is the Gospel of life, and the Gospel of life is the Gospel. The Gospel of life is the *kerygma* and *didache* of the Lord of life. In the words of *Evangelium Vitae*, "Jesus is the only Gospel: We have nothing further to say nor any other witness to bear."

"O Death, Where Is Your Sting?"

VIGEN GUROIAN

The electricity had gone off that evening, and we sat facing one another in pitch darkness at the small kitchen table. A single candle flickered between us. I leaned over toward Kevork in order to listen to the story he was about to tell. "Kevork, you don't have to put yourself through this," I said. "No, Vigen," he answered. "It helps to tell others what happened."

On a sunny December morning in 1988, the earth shook so fiercely in Armenia that the high-rise apartment building in which Kevork, his wife Anahid, and his two children lived, crumbled to the ground. Ten-year-old Armen and his sister Lillit, who was seven, were preparing to leave for school when the floor fell from under them and they were thrust into a black pit, buried beneath ten stories of twisted metal and stone. Kevork raced back home from the school at which he taught. Frantically, he dragged out chunks of shattered concrete from the jagged mountain of wreckage until his hands bled. He crossed the ruined city on foot to find someone with the machinery to dig his children out of their dark Sheol. But for three dreadful days, Armen and Lillit remained wrapped in suffocating darkness, removed from the land of the living. Through it all, Armen courageously encouraged his younger sister to keep hope. On the third day, the rescue team reached the children. Armen died in the hospital two days later: his young body had been crushed from the waist down. Remarkably, Lillit survived, even though she had been pinned to the ground by a steel beam that lodged itself in her forehead.

"I have argued with God day and night," Kevork cried out to me.

118

"But God has not answered! Armen is gone! I will go on living my life in this sorrow, but I am no longer concerned with what God's purposes are or what he can do." "Kevork," I pleaded. "You cannot mean that. Otherwise, why would you keep bringing this up?" Mournfully, the stricken father answered, "Vigen, my friend, what else is left for me?"

Kevork bowed his head. The ensuing silence thickened the surrounding night. Then he looked up, and leaning toward me with his thin sinewy arms, the arms of a man much older than his forty-five years, he asked quietly, "Vigen, you have heard of the Hare Krishna religion? My nephew brought me a book that I want to show to you. In it are drawings about the afterlife and the migrations of the soul. When I was a young man, we were taught in our atheism classes that Marxism is materialist and Christianity is spiritualist. If that is so, Vigen, what is the difference in what I read from this book and what the Bible teaches? Are not both religions spiritualist? I know that Christians believe in resurrection, but can you explain to me how this belief is different from what is shown by the pictures in this book?" "Kevork," I asked. "Do you have a Bible?" He answered, "I do, Vigen, but it is a Russian Bible." Then he added, "I have a dictionary, however. We will manage, Vigen." Kevork got up and disappeared into the darkness. In a few moments, he returned with the book that his nephew had given him, the Russian Bible, and a dictionary that translated from Russian into Armenian. I got out my English Bible and my Armenian-English dictionary.

With these materials spread across the kitchen table, in the candlelight, we began and did not cease until sunrise. Kevork and I read from 1 Corinthians and the last chapter of the Book of Job. But here I am concerned with our conversation about St. Paul's Letter to the Corinthians. I said, "Kevork, St. Paul speaks of resurrection in chapter fifteen. Why don't you read in your Bible while I do the same in mine?" So this Armenian Job read in his Russian Bible and I in mine.

Kevork read very slowly. He read and reread the whole of chapter fifteen. His eyes gaped wide and his lips moved almost rhythmically as he read to himself half aloud. Then his face came aglow, not from the material light but from a light within. He looked up at me, and with a shout he exclaimed: "Vigen, Christianity is materialist! It says we will have bodies! I will see Armen's face again as I see yours now in the candlelight!" What the Hindu doctrine could not promise this broken Armenian father the Bible and Christianity did. My friend was sure that he would see his son again in the kingdom of the Father of all fathers. It was promised.

"Oh Death, where is your sting?
Oh Hades, where is your victory?" (1 Corinthians 15:55)

Kevork and I translated back and forth from Russian to Armenian and Armenian to English and vice versa:

> Behold, I tell you a mystery. We shall not all sleep, but we shall be changed — in a moment, in the twinkling of an eye, at the last trumpet. For the trumpet shall sound, and the dead will be raised incorruptible, and we shall be changed. So when this corruptible [body] has put on incorruption, and this mortal [body] has put on immortality, then shall be brought to pass the saying that is written:
>
> > "Death is swallowed up in victory."
> > "O Death, where is your sting?
> > O Hades, where is your victory?"
>
> > (1 Corinthians 15:51-55)

This is taken from the New King James Version of the Bible. Its rendering "O Hades where is your victory" rather than the more widely accepted: "O Death, where is your victory?" is consistent with the translation from Greek texts embraced by the Eastern churches. St. Paul himself adapted his poem from Hosea 13:14, which may be translated from the Hebrew as: "O Death, where are your plagues? O Sheol, where is your destruction?"

The translation, "O Hades, where is your victory," is taken up in Orthodox liturgy, iconography, and theology. It is understood to reveal that Christ's victory over death is accomplished not only on the cross or by the witness of the empty tomb but also in between Good Friday and Easter Sunday, on Holy Saturday. Indeed, soteriologically Holy Saturday may be the most significant of the three days. This is because on that day Christ descends into Hades, knocks down its gates, and liberates its captives — including all of those men and women since Adam who died a corruptible death. Corruptible death is death that dissolves the body and soul unity of the human person and breaks off communion with God. First Peter states that, "The gospel was proclaimed [by Christ] even to the dead, so that, though they had been judged in the flesh as everyone is judged, they might live in the spirit as God does" (I Peter 4:6). And St. Paul writes in his Letter to the Ephesians, " 'When he ascended on high he made captivity itself a captive; he gave gifts to his people' (Now when it says, 'He ascended,' what does it mean but that he also descended into the lower parts of the earth. He who descended is the same as he who ascended far above all heavens, so that he might fill all things.)" (Ephesians 4:7-10). On Holy Saturday, the Lord of Light and Life descends, this time not from heaven to earth but from earth into the "place" of shadows, into the pit of death. There he overcomes darkness with light and corruptible death with his own immortal life. On this day, the God-man, who is without sin and who on the cross reconciled us with God not only defeats death but rescues Adam and Eve from the pit of sin and corruption and takes them with him to the Kingdom of Light and Life. A Byzantine hymn proclaims: "Today Hell groans and cries aloud: 'My power has been destroyed. I accepted a mortal man as one of the dead; yet I cannot keep Him prisoner, and with Him I shall lose all those over whom I ruled. I held in my power the dead from all ages; but see, he is raising them all.' "[1] In the same manner, St. Ephrem the Syrian, a fourth-century patristic writer, proclaims in one of his hymns: "By death the Living One emptied Sheol. He tore it open and let entire throngs flee from it."[2]

"There he beheld the dragon lurking in the water."

(from the Armenian Rite of Epiphany)

St. John Chrysostom reminds us in a homily on 1 Corinthians 15 that by baptism every Christian makes this journey into Hades with Christ and participates in his victory over death. "For the being baptized and immersed, and then emerging, is a symbol of the descent into hell, and the return thence."[3] Eastern icons of Christ's baptism typically

---

1. *The Lenten Triodion,* tr. Mother Mary and Archimandrate Kallistos Ware (London: Faber and Faber, 1978), 656.

2. *Ephrem the Syrian — Hymns,* tr. Kathleen E. McVey, The Classics of Western Spirituality (Mahwah, NJ: Paulist Press, 1989), 92 ("Hymns on the Nativity," 4).

3. St. John Chrysostom, *The Homilies of St. John Chrysostom on the First Epistle to the Corinthians,* Part 2, A Library of Fathers of the Holy Catholic Church (Oxford: John Henry Parker: London: J. G. F. and J. Rivington, 1839), 572 (Homily 40).

depict the waters of the Jordan in dark shades, so that the river has the appearance of a cave, reminiscent of Hades. Often a serpent or dragon figure is lurking in the water and Christ, who himself is being blessed by John, is blessing the water and transforming it from a liquid tomb into the stream of eternal life. This connection of Christ's and our baptism with Holy Saturday and Christ's descent into Hades is impressively represented in several illuminated miniatures that belong to a fifteenth-century Armenian manuscript of the Four Gospels.[4] It helps to compare the illumination of Christ's Baptism with the two companion folios. One depicts Christ's descent into Hades (usually referred to as the Harrowing of Hell) and the other is a representation of the myrrh-bearing Women at the Empty Tomb. In the East, these two subjects traditionally represent the Resurrection, since the Gospels give no description or explanation of the resurrection event itself.

The simple images of this triptych combine mystagogical, soteriological, and eschatological themes. The painter, a priest named Khatchatur, uses typology and fulfillment, act and eschatology, as richly and effectively and with as much nuance as any written theology. In the miniature of the Baptism, Khatchatur paints Christ in an upright position as he is being blessed by John. But the eyes are drawn into the water by the erect torso, like an arrow pointing downward. Christ is standing on the body of a serpent in the water. One foot is seated on the serpent's head and the other on its neck. The serpent is immobilized, and farther back its snake-like body is twisted into a knot. This, no doubt, is to emphasize that Satan has been confounded and thwarted by Christ.

I have not found these sorts of details in Byzantine icons of the Baptism. Nevertheless, Khatchatur did not invent them. He borrowed from ancient Christian sources, and specifically, I believe, from the great prayer of the blessing of the water of the Armenian Rite of Epiphany. A portion of this prayer states:

> And there [at the Jordan stream] he [Christ] beheld the dread dragon lurking in the water; opening its mouth it was eager to swallow down mankind. . . . But thy only begotten Son by his mighty power trampled the waters under the soles of his feet, sorely punished the

---

4. This manuscript was written and illustrated at the monastery of Gamaghiel at Khizan and is dated 1455. It is owned by the Walter's Art Gallery in Baltimore, Maryland.

mighty brute, according to the prediction of the prophet, that thou hast bruised the head of the dragon upon the waters.[5]

The prophecy is Psalm 74:13-14: "You broke the heads of the sea serpents in the waters./You broke the heads of Leviathan in pieces." This is a text routinely interpreted typologically in Christian exegesis as a prediction of Christ's baptism.

Khatchatur connects the symbolic defeat of Satan in this painting with representations of the Crucifixion, Christ's Harrowing of Hell, the Visit of the Holy Women at the Sepulcher, and the Ascension; but most important for our purpose, with the middle two subjects. In the painting of the Harrowing of Hell, Christ is clad in nail-studded boots. With these boots he is trampling down a prostrate Satan. One foot is on Satan's neck and the other on his rump. Furthermore, the base of the red cross, that he holds, is seated firmly on the head of Satan. The cross alludes to the Crucifixion, but it has been transformed into an unambiguous symbol of victory, quite literally a weapon employed against Satan. The bright red color of the cross might symbolize the Passion, but it is more probably intended as an emblem of royal power. Christ carries the cross in his left hand like a staff or scepter, while he simultaneously pulls Adam and Eve up out of Hades with his right hand. With the same meaning in mind, Georges Florovsky argues that Christ descends into Hades in glory, "not in humiliation, although through humiliation" on the cross.[6]

The miniature of the Holy Women at the Sepulcher deepens this theme of Christ's defeat of death and victory over the demonic powers. The angel, who announces the good news of the resurrection to the three women, is seated on the empty tomb. It is clad in boots, just like those worn by Christ in Hades. With these boots the angel is pushing down the heads and bodies of three demons who are struggling to escape from the nether world from which Christ himself has newly arisen.

At the same time, the angel's head is turned upwards toward the three women who are at the entrance of the cave in the upper left hand corner of the painting. Thus, Khatchatur contrasts the scene at the bottom of the painting with the events above. This suggests the soterio-

---

5. *Rituale Armenorum: The Administration of the Sacrament and Breviary Rites of the Armenian Church*, ed. F. C. Conybeare (Oxford: Clarendon Press, 1905), 168-169.

6. Georges Florovsky, *Creation and Redemption*, vol. 3 of *The Collected Works of Georges Florovsky* (Belmont, MA: Nordland Publishing, 1976), 142.

logical theme of descent and ascent. Opposite the holy women, at the top right of the painting, a risen and glorified Christ stands perfectly upright, just as he is in the painting of the Baptism; only here he is draped in royal garments, matching those worn by Christ in Khatchatur's painting of the Ascension. Christ looks toward the women and blesses them in the trifold manner. In sum, Khatchatur harmonizes the synoptic and Johannine accounts of the discovery of the empty tomb. He combines details from the Gospel narratives as well as from his other paintings in order to signify the singular Christian message of Christ's resurrection and complete triumph over death.

In Orthodox Christianity, iconography and hymnody serve theological and liturgical purposes. We experience the power of this combination of image and word if for a moment we hold in the mind these images and simultaneously listen to the words of the appointed Armenian melodies and ode for Easter Sunday.

Melodies

The voice of good tidings sang to the women.
It sounded like the call of the trumpet: —
"The Crucified whom ye seek is risen!
Fear not but be joyful;
Fulfill what is owed by Eve:
Go to Galilee and see;
And proclaim to the world."

I tell of the voice of the lion
Who roared on the four-winged cross.
On the four-winged cross he roared,
His voice resounded to Hades.

The bird, the bird awoke,
And watching the gentiles,
He called, he called out to the turtle-dove,
To his beloved, nurtured in love.
Love is dawning, love is dawning,
In a stately march it is eagerly rising.
The rising sun, the rising sun —
Such is the name of that daystar.

Mary called to the gardener: —
"Didst thou remove my first-born, my love?"
— "That bird is risen, the wakeful being,"
Did the seraph trumpet to the mother and those with her,
— "The Savior of the world, Christ is risen!
And he delivereth mankind from death."

Ode

On the sepulcher of the immortal who is risen
On this day the heavenly angel cried aloud:
Christ did arise, Christ did awake,
Out of the virgin tomb, out of the tomb of light. . . .
By the holy stone sat the marvelous one and cried aloud,
And the oil-bearing women announced joyfully:
Christ did arise, Christ did awake,
Out of the new tomb, out of the virgin tomb.[7]

"By thy burial we are set free from death."

(from the Byzantine Matins for Holy Saturday)

In his commentary on the Nicene Creed, the late Fr. Alexander Schmemann writes: "We instinctively ask ourselves: why is this word [buried] used, and not the word 'died' "[8] in the Creed. "And he was . . . crucified and suffered and was buried," the Creed states. Schmemann proposes that burial is "an affirmation of a particular understanding of death." In the Christian faith burial points to things and actions that occur after death. In the case of the death of Jesus Christ this means that "He, who is life itself, descends to death out of love and co-suffering, descends to a death which he did not create, which has taken over the world and poisoned life."[9] The Life of life dies willingly in order to overcome mortality and corruptible death. The new Adam rescues us from the condition of mortality in which we

7. *Divine Liturgy of the Armenian Apostolic Church*, tr. Tiran Abp. Nersoyan, 5th edition (London: St. Sarkis Church, 1984), 141-142 (Variables for the Principal Feast Days).

8. Alexander Schmemann, *The Celebration of Faith*, Sermons, vol. 1 (Crestwood, NY: St. Vladimir's Seminary Press, 1991), 86.

9. Schmemann, *Celebration of Faith*, 88.

were left by the old Adam's sin. The Son of God brings light, his own immaterial light, to the dead who are covered in darkness and subject to the worm. And when he raised "up the dead from the dwelling place beneath the earth, all the powers of heaven cried aloud: 'Giver of Life, O Christ, glory to Thee.'"[10]

In a Byzantine hymn for Holy Saturday Christ speaks from out of the grave to comfort his mother and the other women who had hastened to visit the tomb in the morning:

> "By mine own will this earth covers Me, O Mother, but the gatekeepers of hell tremble as they see Me, clothed in the bloodstained garment of vengeance: for on the Cross as God have I struck down Mine enemies, and I shall rise again. . . .
>
> "Let the creation rejoice exceedingly, let all those born on earth be glad: for hell, the enemy, has been despoiled. Ye women, come to meet Me with sweet spices: for I am delivering Adam and Eve with all their offspring, and on the third day I will rise."[11]

This is the One who also announces to the seer of the Book of Revelation: " 'Do not be afraid; I am the First and the Last. I am He who lives, and was dead, and behold, I am alive forever more. Amen. And I have the keys of Hades and of Death' " (Rev. 1:10, 17-18).

In other religions death is greeted as the immortal soul's great liberator from earthly captivity and woe. In the Christian faith, however, death is the great despoiler of the creature whom God has made in his very own image. The human person is not just a soul, for then he would be a ghost; nor is he simply a physical body, for then he would be a corpse. The human person is a body and soul unity, and death tears that unity asunder. That is the meaning of what the ancient fathers call corruptible death. And that is what my friend Kevork sought an answer to. It was his own flesh and blood that had been crushed under the concrete and steel and it was that flesh and blood that he yearned to see and embrace once again. St. Paul promised what the Hare Krishna religion could not, that the dead person would be made whole again, not that the soul would go on existing in some other form or in some nebulous nether world, but that this very same corruptible [body] would . . . put on incorruption and this mortal [body] . . . immortality" (1 Cor. 15:53).

---

10. *Lenten Triodion*, 622.
11. *Lenten Triodion*, 651.

"If men's bodies are to be detained in the earth," writes St. John Chrysostom, "it follows that the tyranny of death remains. . . . But if this, which Paul spake of, ensue, as undoubtedly it will ensue, God's victory will appear, and that a glorious one, in His Being able to raise again the bodies which were hidden thereby."[12]

My friend Kevork comprehended this Christian truth about the promise of resurrection, and he greeted it with a shout of joy. I often tell the story of that night of discovery and revelation to my college students. I do so because of the profound confusion about Christian belief that so many of them carry about. Many who regard themselves as Christians do not comprehend or believe what Kevork discovered and rejoiced in. Many do not believe in the resurrection of the body. As Schmemann rightly observes: "In the real life of contemporary Christianity and Christians, faith in the resurrection has very little place, however strange that may sound." Ask a contemporary church-goer what he really thinks about death and "you will hear some vague, and still pre-Christian idea about the immortality of the soul and its life in some sort of world beyond the grave."[13] This Christian may even affirm that Christ rose bodily and still believe that what awaits us is an immortal existence of the soul.

The Orthodox theology of Holy Saturday corrects that mistake in an unexpected but nevertheless very powerful way. Christ's post-resurrection appearances, especially his encounter with Thomas who doubted, have been invoked countless times to correct the neo-Hellenization of the Christian faith. But these stories are about *Christ* and about *his* resurrected body. Holy Saturday is about our destinies. Hades is a place of dread because it is a "place of . . . disembodiment and disincarnation,"[14] a shadowy, spectral realm, and insubstantial. Christ's descent into Hades is not only the precondition of his own bodily resurrection but of ours as well. Here we need to note that Hades is not the same as the hell of suffering and torment that would be inhabited by unrepentant sinners. The latter is a function or product of the Incarnation and Resurrection. It is only with respect to Christ's birth, death, and resurrection, in other words God's work of redemption in and through his only begotten Son, that Hell as a

12. John Chrysostom, *Homilies on the First Epistle to the Corinthians*, 562 (Homily 39).

13. Schmemann, *Celebration of Faith*, 90.

14. Florovsky, *Creation and Redemption*, 141.

"state" of "eternal" reprobation of the unrepentant is possible. But this is a difficult and immense topic.

What needs to be said here is that on Holy Saturday, Hades is abolished once and for all. We are speaking in the language of myth. Through mythopoeic imagery we may grasp the soteriologic truth that corruptible, disincarnate death is no longer our interminable fate but is replaced by bodily resurrection and eternal life. With this meaning in mind, Georges Florovsky insists that, "the descent into hell [or Hades] is already the resurrection."[15]

Christ's death was a real human death; but because he was the incarnate Word of God and was without sin there was no inherent necessity in his death. His death was *not* a corruptible death, nor did his body decay in the grave. In an act of immeasurable and redeeming love, the incarnate Word, the immortal Lord of life, accepted death freely and willingly and thus overcame corruptible death in our body, in the humanity that he bore with him on the cross and into Hades and back to his Father in heaven. When Jesus died on the cross, his body and soul were separated. Nevertheless, they remained in unbroken communication through the power of the Hypostatic Union. St. Gregory of Nyssa explains this: "When our nature, following its own course, had even in Him been advanced to the separation of soul and body, He knitted together again the disunited elements, cementing them, as it were, together with the cement of His divine power, and recombining what has been severed in a reunion never to be broken. And this is the Resurrection."[16]

Likewise, Christ's human death did not separate him from the enlivening love of the Father and the Holy Spirit. "In the Grave with the body, and in Hades with the soul, in that thou art God; in Paradise with the thief, and on the throne with the Father and the Spirit, in that thou art infinite,"[17] declares a Paschal hymn of the Orthodox Church. In other words, the divine Hypostasis, who is the incarnate Word, never loses his divine and human identity, not even in death. Jesus, who was crucified, died, and was buried, is the very same one

15. Florovsky, *Creation and Redemption*, 139.

16. Gregory of Nyssa, *The Great Catechism*, in *A Select Library of Nicene and Post-Nicene Fathers of the Christian Church*, 2nd ser., vol. 5 (Grand Rapids: Eerdmans, 1979), 489.

17. *Service Book of the Holy Orthodox-Catholic Apostolic Church*, ed. and tr. Isabel Florence Hapgood (Englewood, NJ: Antiochian Orthodox Christian Archdiocese, 1975), 237.

who descends into Hades and ascends to the Father. We narrate these "events" in terms of temporal chronology. But, in truth, even as he descends into Hades and lies bodily in the grave, Christ is with the thief in Paradise and on the throne of the Father with the Spirit. Christians say and mean the same when they state that the Son is with the Father in heaven and yet is present through the power of the Spirit in the elements at the eucharistic table.

"The last enemy to be destroyed is death."

(1 Corinthians 15:26)

With the rising of the sun came a new day, and early on that day Kevork drove me to Armen's grave. Printed on the great polished granite stone was a nearly life-sized photograph of Armen. Kevork dropped to his knees in prayer and then with a care so intense that it created its own dense atmosphere, as incense at the altar, he slowly, reverently wiped the entire surface of the gravestone with a new white handkerchief. The polished stone shone bright in the noon-day sun, and the father, with eyes washed in tears, sighed a deep sigh.

I looked around me at all of the other new gravestones. Leninakan — which today has been returned to its ancient name of Giumri — was a city of some two hundred thousand when the earthquake struck. More than fifteen thousand persons perished when the earth trembled on that December day. Their gravestones populated whole hillsides — entire families buried next to one another — a city of the dead, waiting, waiting for the sound of the trumpet, the last call, and resurrection. What does St. Paul say? "For the trumpet will sound, and the dead will be raised incorruptible, and we shall be changed." But what kind of a hope is this, this resurrection hope, if not something more than the hope of my own individual immortality? What good would such an immortality be without the presence of the others whom I loved in life and who loved me? As I looked out on this city of graves, I began to realize in my gut and not just my intellect that Holy Saturday is compelling for Orthodox Christians because of its profound social meaning, because through its symbolism the victory of Christ over death is made tangible as a communal event. Christ's descent into Hades is a triumph over the desolation and the loneliness, the isolation and the despair, that Satan, sin, and death have inflicted

upon every human being. The iconography testifies to this social sote-
riology.

In a wonderful study of Eastern iconography, entitled simply
enough *The Art of the Icon: A Theology of Beauty*, Paul Evdokimov discusses a fourteenth-century painting of the Descent into Hades that
still exists in the chapel of the Church of the Holy Savior of Chora in
Constantinople. It is a painting filled with persons and movement.
And it dramatically portrays this social character of the Christian belief in resurrection. Evdokimov writes:

> In a powerful hand movement, Christ yanks bewildered Adam and
> Eve from Hades. We have here the *powerful meeting of the two Adams*
> and a foretelling of the fullness of the Kingdom. The two Adams are
> together and identify one another, no longer in the *kenosis* of the In-
> carnation, but in the Glory of the Parousia. "He who said to Adam
> 'Where are you?' has mounted the Cross to search for him who was
> lost. He went down into Hades saying: Come to me my image and
> likeness" (a hymn by St. Ephrem). This is why the groups on the left
> and the right are in the background; they are the constitutive ele-
> ments of Adam, that is, all humanity, individual men and women.
> They are the righteous and the prophets. On the left are the kings Da-
> vid and Solomon; they are preceded by the Forerunner whose gesture
> calls attention and points to the Savior. On the right is Moses who of-
> ten carries the Tablets of the Law. All recognize the Savior and ex-
> press their recognition by their gestures and attitudes.[18]

"True heavenly bliss is impossible for me if I isolate myself from
the world-whole and care about myself only,"[19] wrote the great twentieth-century Russian religious philosopher Nicholas Berdyaev. Satan
prompts us to be this way and would seal our fate were it not for the
victory that the Son of God accomplishes over sin and death. If Hades
is the shadow of isolation and desolation cast by sin, then the descent
of the Creator and the Savior of the world into Hades and his rescue of
its inhabitants is that deed by which is begun the gathering in and reunion of all of Adam's seed into the communion of the Kingdom of
Love. A prayer of the Armenian burial service poignantly expresses

18. Paul Evdokimov, *The Art of the Icon: A Theology of Beauty* (Redondo Beach, CA:
Oakwood Publications, 1990), 325.
19. Nicholas Berdyaev, *The Destiny of Man* (New York: Harper and Row, 1960), 294.

this hope and expectation: "Our Father . . . thou hast vouchsafed unto us a place of rest from our earthly toils, the painless and the toilless life. Thou through thy only-begotten Son hast slain death and hast illumined this life and incorruptibility. And thou hast saved the holy ones from the dominion of darkness, and hast transferred them to the kingdom of thy beloved Son our Lord and Savior Jesus Christ."[20]

This final victory over death that St. Paul proclaims is a triumph of communion over isolation and of love over desolation. "To earth Thou didst come down, O master, to save Adam: and not finding him on earth, Thou hast descended into hell, seeking him there. . . . Uplifted on the Cross, Thou hast uplifted with Thyself all living men; and then descending beneath the earth, Thou raisest all that lie buried there."[21]

That evening, there was a humble supper at Kevork's home. Family and friends gathered. We cooked kebab on a grill, while others brought sweets and drink. It was not the great wedding feast. But it *was* a foretaste of that heavenly banquet. Even amidst the sorrows of our greatest losses in life, God permits us to taste of the kingdom of heaven. In his great catechetical address, which is said at every Byzantine Easter matins service, St. John Chrysostom proclaims:

> Enter you all into the joy of your Lord; and receive your reward. . . . The table is full-laden; feast you all sumptuously. Enjoy you all the feast of faith: Receive you all the riches of loving-kindness. . . . Let no one fear death, for the savior's death hath set us free. . . . O Death were is thy sting? O Hell, where is thy victory? Christ is risen and thou art overthrown. Christ is risen, and the demons are fallen. Christ is risen, and the Angels rejoice. Christ is risen, and life reigneth. Christ is risen, and not one dead remaineth in the grave.[22]

20. *Rituale Armenorum*, 121.
21. *Lenten Triodion*, 625, 627.
22. *Service Book of the Holy Orthodox-Catholic Apostolic Church*, 235.

Contributors

GARY A. ANDERSON, Professor of Hebrew Bible, Harvard Divinity School, Cambridge, Massachusetts

CARL E. BRAATEN, Executive Director, Center for Catholic and Evangelical Theology; Co-Editor, *Pro Ecclesia*

VIGEN GUROIAN, Professor of Theology and Ethics, Loyola College in Maryland, Baltimore, Maryland

STANLEY HAUERWAS, Gilbert T. Rowe Professor of Theological Ethics, The Divinity School, Duke University, Durham, North Carolina

ROBERT W. JENSON, Senior Scholar for Research, Center of Theological Inquiry, Princeton, New Jersey; Co-Editor, *Pro Ecclesia*

GILBERT MEILAENDER, Board of Directors Chair in Theological Ethics, Valparaiso University, Valparaiso, Indiana

RICHARD JOHN NEUHAUS, President, The Institute on Religion and Public Life, New York, New York; Editor-in-Chief, *First Things*

A. N. WILLIAMS, Assistant Professor, The Walter H. Gray Chair of Anglican Studies, The Divinity School, Yale University, New Haven, Connecticut